Rick Steves' ®

SNAPSHOT

Loire
Valley

D0288919

CONTENTS

INTRODUCTION

This Snapshot guide, excerpted from the latest edition of my guidebook *Rick Steves' France*, is all about the Loire Valley. What was once the preserve of French aristocracy is now a playground for commoners like us. Exquisite châteaux dot the lush landscape of the Loire Valley like jewels in a crown—I cover 15 of my favorites. Chenonceau delights with its dramatic setting atop a river, while the king's "hunting lodge" at Chambord astonishes with 440 rooms—and almost as many chimneys. The best gardens are at Villandry, while Cheverny has the most impressive furnishings—and a fun daily feeding of its hunting hounds. When you need a break, rise above it all in a hot-air balloon or get a feel for the countryside by renting a bike. A visit to "the garden of France" confirms why the Loire Valley was royalty's number-one getaway.

To help you have the best trip possible, I've included the following topics in this book:

• **Planning Your Time,** with advice on how to make the most of your limited time

• **Orientation,** including tourist information (abbreviated as TI), tips on public transportation, local tour options, and helpful hints

• **Sights** with ratings:

▲▲▲—Don't miss

▲▲—Try hard to see

▲—Worthwhile if you can make it

No rating—Worth knowing about

• **Sleeping** and **Eating,** with good-value recommendations in every price range

• **Connections,** with tips on trains, buses, and driving

• **Practicalities,** near the end of this book, has information on money, phoning, hotel reservations, transportation, and more, plus French survival phrases.

To travel smartly, read this little book in its entirety before you go. It's my hope that this guide will make your trip more meaningful and rewarding. Traveling like a temporary local, you'll get the absolute most out of every mile, minute, and euro.

Bon voyage!

Rick Steves

THE LOIRE

Amboise • Chinon • Beaucoup de Châteaux

As it glides gently east to west, officially separating northern from southern France, the Loire River has come to define this popular tourist region. The importance of this river and the valley's prime location, in the center of the country just south of Paris, have made the Loire a strategic hot potato for more than a thousand years. Because of its history, this region is home to more than a thousand castles and palaces in all shapes and sizes. When a "valley address" became a must-have among 16th-century hunting-crazy royalty, rich Renaissance palaces replaced outdated medieval castles.

Hundreds of these castles and palaces are open to visitors, and it's castles that you're here to see (you'll find better villages and cities elsewhere). Old-time aristocratic château-owners, struggling with the cost of upkeep, enjoy financial assistance from the government if they open their mansions to the public.

Today's Loire Valley is carpeted with fertile fields, crisscrossed by rivers, and laced with rolling hills. It's one of France's most important agricultural regions. It's also under some development pressure, thanks to TGV bullet trains that link it to Paris in an hour, and cheap flights to England that make it a prime second-home spot for many Brits, including Sir Mick Jagger.

Choosing a Home Base

This is a big, unwieldy region for travelers, so I've divided it into two halves, each centered around a good, manageable town to use as a base: Amboise or Chinon. Châteaux-holics and gardeners can stay longer and sleep in both towns. Amboise is east of the big city of Tours, and Chinon lies to Tours' west. The drive from Amboise to Chinon is more than an hour; if you sleep on one side of Tours and intend to visit castles on the other side, you're looking at a long round-trip drive—certainly doable, but not my idea of good travel. Instead, sleep in or near the town nearest the castles you plan to visit, and avoid crossing the traffic-laden city of Tours. The A-85 autoroute is the quickest way to link Amboise with châteaux near Chinon. Thanks to this uncrowded freeway, little Azay-le-Rideau is another good base for destinations west of Tours, and also works as a base for sights on both sides of Tours.

Amboise is the best home base for first-timers to this area, as it offers handy access to these important châteaux: Chenonceau, Blois, Chambord, Cheverny, Fougères-sur-Bièvre, Chaumont-sur-Loire, Loches, and Valençay. Amboise also has better train connections from Paris and better public transportation options to nearby sights, making it the preferable choice if you don't want to rent a car or bike.

Chinon, Azay-le-Rideau, and their nearby châteaux don't feel as touristy, and appeal to gardeners and road-less-traveled types. The key sights in this area include the châteaux of Chinon, Azay-le-Rideau, Langeais, Villandry, Chatonnière, Rivau, Ussé, and the Abbaye Royale de Fontevraud. Chinon and Azay-le-Rideau are also optimal for cyclists, with quicker access to bike paths and more interesting destinations within pedaling distance.

Loches is a more remote home-base option for drivers, who should also consider the tempting rural accommodations listed throughout this chapter.

Planning Your Time

With frequent, convenient trains to Paris and a few direct runs to Charles de Gaulle Airport, the Loire can be a good first or last stop on your French odyssey (more than 20 trains/day between Paris' Gare Montparnasse or Gare d'Austerlitz and Amboise, 1.5-2 hours; some trains from Gare d'Austerlitz require an easy transfer in Blois or Les Aubrais-Orléans, and all trains from Montparnasse require a change in St. Pierre-des-Corps; 6 trains/day between Charles de Gaulle Airport and Tours, 2 hours; easy car rental at St. Pierre-des-Corps Station, 15 minutes from Amboise).

A day and a half is sufficient to sample the best châteaux. Don't go overboard. Two châteaux, possibly three (if you're a big person), make up the recommended daily dosage. Famous châteaux are least crowded early and late in the day. Most open at about 9:00 and close between 18:00 and 19:00. During the off-season, some close at 17:00 and midday from 12:00 to 14:00. The Festival of Gardens at Chaumont runs May to mid-October from 10:00 to 20:00.

Drivers: For the single best day in the Loire, consider this

THE LOIRE

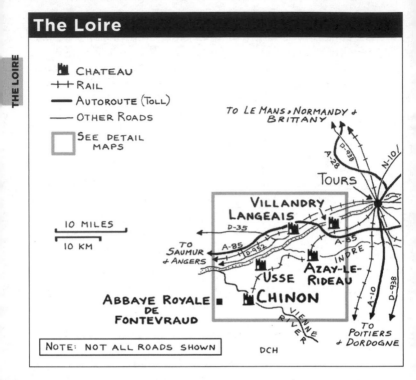

The Loire

Legend:
- Chateau
- Rail
- Autoroute (Toll)
- Other Roads
- See Detail Maps

10 MILES
10 KM

TO LE MANS, NORMANDY & BRITTANY

TOURS

VILLANDRY
LANGEAIS
D-35

TO SAUMUR & ANGERS

A-85
D-952

USSE
AZAY-LE-RIDEAU

INDRE

ABBAYE ROYALE DE FONTEVRAUD

CHINON

VIENNE RIVER

TO POITIERS & DORDOGNE

A-10
D-938

NOTE: NOT ALL ROADS SHOWN

DCH

plan: Sleep in or near Amboise and visit Chenonceau early (arrive by 9:00), when crowds are small; spend midday at Chambord (30-minute drive from Chenonceau); and enjoy Chaumont or Cheverny on the way back to your hotel (the hunting dogs are fed at 17:00 on most days at Cheverny). Remember to allow time to visit Amboise. With a second full day, move to Chinon, visiting Villandry and Langeais en route, then devote your afternoon to Chinon.

The best map of the area is Michelin #518, covering all the sights described in this chapter (the TI's free map of Touraine, the area surrounding Tours, is also good).

Try to see one château on your drive in (for example, if arriving from the north, visit Chambord, Cheverny, or Blois; if coming from the west or the south, see Azay-le-Rideau, Chinon, Langeais, or Villandry). If you're coming from Burgundy, don't miss the remarkable Château de Guédelon. If you're driving to the Dordogne from the Loire, the A-20 autoroute via Limoges (near Oradour-sur-Glane) is fastest and toll-free until Brive-la-Gaillarde.

Without a Car: On a tight budget, bike or catch the public bus, a shuttle van (summers only), or the train from Amboise to the

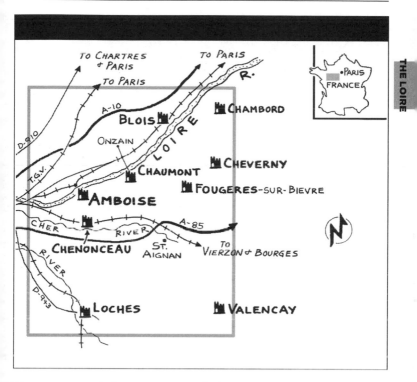

town of Chenonceaux, tour Chenonceau (the château), then spend the afternoon enjoying Amboise, its château, and Leonardo's last stand at Clos-Lucé. With a second day, the best (but pricier) option is a minivan excursion directly from Amboise to Chambord and Cheverny. If you're watching your wallet, take the train to Blois, tour its castle and old town, then take the excursion bus (runs April-early Sept) or taxi from there to Chambord and Cheverny. (For more train and bus specifics, see "Amboise Connections" on page 32 and "Blois Connections" on page 46.) Those connecting Paris with Amboise or Chinon can lay over in Blois en route (baggage check available at château). Budget travelers based in Chinon can bike to Langeais, Ussé, and Villandry, and/or take the train to Azay-le-Rideau and Langeais (the train trips are long, and not a good option for most).

A limited visit to the Loire is doable as a day trip from Paris. Several minivan and bus tours make getting to the main châteaux a breeze (see "By Bus, Minivan Excursion, or Taxi" later).

Getting Around the Loire Valley

If you're looking to hunt down remote châteaux, rent a car. Day rentals are easy in Amboise and at the St. Pierre-des-Corps train station in Tours (but not in Chinon). Trains, buses, minivan tours, bikes, or taxis help non-drivers reach the well-known châteaux (all described later). To get to the less-famous châteaux without a car, you can take a taxi, arrange for a custom minivan excursion (affordable for small groups), or ride a bike (great option for those with enough time and stamina).

By Train

With easy access from Amboise and Chinon, the big city of Tours is the transport hub for travelers bent on using the train or buses to explore the Loire (but it has little else to offer visitors—I wouldn't sleep there). Tours has two important train stations and a major bus station (with service to several châteaux). The main train station is called Tours SNCF, and the smaller, suburban TGV Station (located between Tours and Amboise) is St. Pierre-des-Corps. Check the schedules carefully, as service is sparse on some lines. The châteaux of Amboise, Blois, Chenonceau, Chaumont (via the town of Onzain plus a long walk), Langeais, Chinon, and Azay-le-Rideau have train and/or bus service from Tours' Main (SNCF) Station; Amboise, Blois, Chaumont, and Chenonceau are also served from Tours' St. Pierre-des-Corps Station. Look under each sight for specifics, and seriously consider a minivan excursion (described next).

By Bus, Minivan Excursion, or Taxi

A few bus and shuttle van routes and minivan excursions offer painless transportation to the valley's châteaux. These organized itineraries make life far easier for those without a car, and can save you time (in line) and money (on admissions) when you purchase your château ticket at a discounted group rate from the driver. TIs in the region have details on the options listed here, and on others offering similar services.

Although the minivan companies don't visit all the castles in this chapter, they organize custom excursions, and will pick up your small group in Amboise, Chinon, or Azay-le-Rideau (€20-35/person for scheduled half-day itineraries from Tours, €45-50 for all day; figure €220 for custom groups of up to 7 for 4 hours, €390 all day).

From Amboise to East of Tours

This area's three big-name castles—Chenonceau, Chambord, and Cheverny—are reachable by bus or shuttle van; minivan tours offer visits to the same three, and quick glances at a few others.

By Bus: If you're on a budget and visiting in high season, the region's buses are workable. A handy excursion bus departs from the Blois train station—an easy train ride from Amboise—and runs a loop route connecting Blois, Chambord, Cheverny, and (skip-pable) Beauregard, allowing visits to the châteaux with your pick of return times. This service runs from April until early September (see "Blois Connections," page 46). Buses also connect Amboise and Chenonceaux (1-2/day; see "Amboise Connections," page 32).

By Shuttle Van: Quart de Tours runs a summer-only van service between Amboise and the Château de Chenonceau, and between Amboise, Chambord, and Cheverny (see "Amboise Connections," page 32).

By Minivan Excursion: Acco-Dispo is a small, well-run minibus company based in Amboise with good all-day château tours from Amboise and Tours. Costs vary with the itinerary (from Amboise—€34/half-day, €52/day; from Tours—€20/half-day, €50/day; daily, free hotel pickups, 18 rue des Vallées, Amboise, tel. 06 82 00 64 51, fax 02 47 57 67 13, www.accodispo-tours.com). English is the primary language. While on the road, you'll usually get a fun and enthusiastic running commentary covering each châ-teau's background, as well as the region's contemporary scene—but you're on your own at each château. (You're responsible for entry fees but can buy tickets from the driver at group rates—a good sav-ings.) All-day tours depart 8:30-10:30 (varies by itinerary); after-noon tours depart 13:20-13:50. Both return to Amboise at about 18:30. Several itineraries are available; most include Chenonceau, and some throw in a wine-tasting. If possible, reserve a week ahead by email, or two or three days ahead by phone. Groups are small, ranging from two to eight château-hoppers. (Day-trippers from Paris find this service convenient; after a one-hour TGV ride to Tours, you're met near the central station and returned there at day's end.) Acco-Dispo also runs multiday tours of the Loire and Brittany.

Another minivan option, **Loire Valley Tours** offers all-day itineraries from Amboise to either châteaux near Amboise or châ-teaux near Chinon. The tours are fully guided and include admis-sions, lunch, and wine-tasting (about €135/person, tel. 02 54 33 99 80, www.loire-valley-tours.com, contact@loire-valley-tours.com).

By Taxi: Taxi excursions from the Blois train station to nearby châteaux can be affordable when split among several people. For details, see "Blois Connections," page 46, or call the Blois TI at tel. 02 54 90 41 41.

From Chinon to Châteaux West of Tours

Tours is a one-hour train ride from Chinon (12 trains or SNCF buses/day). Minivan excursions leave from Tours' TI to many châ-teaux, including Azay-le-Rideau and Villandry. Try **Acco-Dispo** or **Quart de Tours,** with daily three-hour tours to Azay-le-Rideau and Villandry for about €22 (both companies described earlier).

THE LOIRE

Loire Valley Châteaux at a Glance

Which châteaux should you visit—and why? Here's a quick summary. Remember, TIs sell bundled tickets for several châteaux that save you money and time in ticket lines (see page 16).

Châteaux East of Tours

▲▲▲**Chenonceau** For sheer elegance arching over the Cher River, and for its lovely gardens. **Hours:** Daily mid-March-mid-Sept 9:00-19:00, July-Aug until 20:00, closes earlier off-season. See page 36.

▲▲**Blois** For its urban setting, beautiful courtyard, and fun sound-and-light show. **Hours:** Daily July-Aug 9:00-19:00, April-June and Sept 9:00-18:30, Oct 9:00-17:30, Nov-March 9:00-12:30 & 14:00-17:30. See page 41.

▲▲**Chambord** For its grandeur (440 rooms), fun rooftop views, and evocative setting surrounded by a forest. **Hours:** Daily April-Sept 9:00-18:15, Oct-March 9:00-17:15. See page 47.

▲▲**Cheverny** For its intimate feel, lavishly furnished rooms, and daily feeding of the hunting dogs. **Hours:** Daily July-Aug 9:15-19:00, April-June and Sept 9:15-18:15, Oct 9:45-17:30, Nov-March 9:45-17:00. See page 50.

▲▲**Chaumont-sur-Loire** For its imposing setting over the Loire River, intriguing rooms, and impressive Festival of the Gardens. **Hours:** Daily July-Aug 10:00-19:00, May-June and early Sept 10:00-18:00, April and late Sept 10:30-17:30, Oct-March 10:00-17:00. See page 53.

▲**Amboise** For terrific views over Amboise and Leonardo da Vinci memories. **Hours:** Daily April-June 9:00-18:30, July-Aug 9:00-19:00, Sept-Oct and March 9:00-18:00, Nov-Jan 9:00-12:00 & 14:00-16:45, Feb 9:00-12:00 & 13:30-17:30. See page 19.

▲**Clos-Lucé (in Amboise)** For a chance to see Leonardo da Vinci's final home, and to stroll through gardens decorated with models of his creations. **Hours:** Daily April-Oct 9:00-19:00, Nov-Dec and Feb-March 9:00-18:00, Jan 9:00-17:00. See page 20.

Fougères-sur-Bièvre For its medieval architecture and presentation of castle-construction techniques. **Hours:** May-mid-Sept daily 9:30-12:30 & 14:00-18:30; mid-Sept-April Wed-Mon 10:00-12:00 & 14:00-17:00, closed Tue. See page 52.

Valençay For its Renaissance design, lovely gardens, and kid-friendly summer events. **Hours:** Daily June 9:30-18:30, July-Aug 9:30-19:00, April-May and Sept 10:00-18:00, Oct 10:20-17:30, closed Nov-March. See page 56.

Châteaux West of Tours
▲▲**Azay-le-Rideau** For its fairy-tale facade and setting on a romantic reflecting pond, and for its beautifully furnished rooms. **Hours:** Daily July-Aug 9:30-19:00, April-June and Sept-Oct 9:30-18:00, Nov-March 10:00-12:30 & 14:00-17:30. See page 68.

▲▲**Villandry** For the best gardens in the Loire Valley. **Hours:** Daily April-Sept 9:00-19:00, March and Oct 9:00-18:00, Nov-Feb 9:00-17:00. See page 71.

▲**Chinon** For its Joan of Arc history. **Hours:** Daily May-Aug 9:30-19:00, April and Sept 9:30-18:00, Oct-March 9:30-17:00. See page 60.

▲**Langeais** For its fortress-like setting above an appealing little village, and its 16th-century furnished rooms. **Hours:** Daily July-Aug 9:00-19:00, April-June and Sept-mid-Nov 9:30-18:30, mid Nov-March 10:00-17:00. See page 69.

Château de Chatonnière For its overflowing flower display in spring and early summer. **Hours:** Daily mid-March-mid-Nov 10:00-19:00. See page 73.

Château du Rivau For its lovely vegetable and flower gardens based on designs from medieval tapestries. **Hours:** Daily April-Sept 10:00-18:00, Oct-mid-Nov 10:00-12:30 & 14:00-18:00, closed mid-Nov-March. See page 73.

Ussé For an exterior look at its architecture, which inspired the romantic Sleeping Beauty story. **Hours:** Daily April-Aug 10:00-19:00, mid-Feb-March and Sept-mid-Nov 10:00-18:00, closed mid-Nov-mid-Feb. See page 73.

Touraine Evasion offers similar services and prices with an audioguide (tel. 06 07 39 13 31, www.tourevasion.com).

By Bike

Cycling options are endless in the Loire, where the elevation gain is generally manageable. (However, if you have only a day or two, rent a car or stick to the châteaux easily reached by buses and mini-vans.) Amboise, Blois, Azay-le-Rideau, and Chinon all make good biking bases and have rental options. A network of nearly 200 miles of bike paths and well-signed country lanes connect many châteaux near Amboise. Pick up the free bike-path map at any TI, buy the more detailed map available at TIs, or study the route options at www.loireavelo.fr. (I also list several accommodations with easy access to these bike paths.)

Near Chinon, a 30-mile bike path runs along the Loire River, passing by Ussé and Langeais, then meeting the Cher River at Villandry and continuing along the Cher to Tours and beyond. To follow this route, pick up the *La Loire à Vélo* brochure at any area TI.

Tours-based **Detours du Loire** can help you plan your bike route and will deliver rental bikes to most places in the Loire for reasonable rates (35 rue Charles-Gilles, tel. 02 47 61 22 23, www.locationdevelos.com). Bikes are available to rent in Amboise, Chenonceaux, Blois, Azay-Le-Rideau, and Chinon (ask at the TI in each city for bike rental shops).

By Car

You can rent a car most easily at Tours' St. Pierre-des-Corps train station, or in Amboise. I've listed specific driving instructions for each destination covered in this chapter.

The Loire Valley's Cuisine Scene

Here in "the garden of France," locally produced food is delicious. Loire Valley rivers yield fresh trout *(truite),* salmon *(saumon),* and smelt *(éperlau),* which are often served fried *(friture). Rillettes,* a stringy pile of cooked and whipped pork, makes for a cheap, mouthwatering sandwich spread (use lots of mustard and add a baby pickle, called a *cornichon).* The area's wonderful goat cheeses include Crottin de Chavignol *(crottin* means horse dung, which is what this cheese, when aged, resembles), Saint-Maure Fermier (soft and creamy), and Selles-sur-Cher (mild). For dessert, try a delicious *tarte tatin* (upside-down caramel-apple tart).

Remember, restaurants serve food only during lunch (11:30-14:00) and dinner (19:00-21:00, later in bigger cities); bigger cafés offer eats throughout the day.

Hot-Air Balloon Rides

In France's most popular regions, you'll find hot-air balloon companies eager to take you for a ride (Burgundy, the Loire, Dordogne, and Provence are best suited for ballooning). It's not cheap, but it's unforgettable—a once-in-a-lifetime chance to sail serenely over châteaux, canals, vineyards, Romanesque churches, and villages. Balloons don't go above 3,000 feet and usually fly much lower than that, so you get a bird's-eye view of France's sublime landscapes.

Most companies offer similar deals and work this way: Trips range from 45 to 90 minutes of air time, to which you must add two hours for preparation, champagne toast, and transport back to your starting point. Deluxe trips add a gourmet picnic, making it a four-hour event. Allow about €190 for a short tour, and about €270 for longer flights. Departures are, of course, weather-dependent, and are usually scheduled first thing in the morning or in early evening. If you've booked ahead and the weather turns bad, you can reschedule your flight, but you can't get your money back. Most balloon companies charge about €25 more for a bad-weather refund guarantee; unless your itinerary is very loose, it's a good idea.

Flight season is April through October. It's smart to bring a jacket for the breeze, though temperatures in the air won't differ too much from those on the ground. Air sickness is usually not a problem, as the ride is typically slow and even. Baskets have no seating, so count on standing the entire trip. Group (and basket) size can vary from 4 to 16 passengers. Area TIs have brochures. **France Montgolfières** gets good reviews and offers flights in the areas that I recommend (tel. 02 54 32 20 48, fax 02 54 32 20 07, www.france-mont golfiere.com). Others are **Aérocom Montgolfière** (tel. 02 54 33 55 00, www.aerocom.fr) and **Touraine Montgolfière** (tel. 02 47 56 42 05, www.touraine-montgolfiere.fr).

Wines of the Loire

Loire wines are overlooked, and that's a shame—there is gold in them thar grapes. The Loire is France's third-largest producer of wine and grows the greatest variety of any region. Four main grapes are grown in the Loire: two reds, Gamay and Cabernet Franc, and two whites, Sauvignon Blanc and Chenin Blanc.

The Loire is divided into four subareas, and the name of a wine (its *appellation*) generally refers to where its grapes were grown. The Touraine subarea encompasses the wines of Chinon and Amboise. Using 100 percent Cabernet Franc grapes, growers in Chinon and Bourgeuil are the main (and best) producers of reds. Thanks to soil variation and climate differences year in and out, wines made from a single grape have a remarkable range in taste. The best and most expensive white wines are the Sancerres, made on the less-touristed western edge of the Loire. Less expensive, but still tasty, are Touraine Sauvignons and the sweeter Vouvray, whose grapes are grown near Amboise. Vouvray is also famous for its light and refreshing sparkling wines (called *vins pétillants*)—locals will tell you the only proper way to begin any meal in this region is with a glass of it, and I can't disagree (try the *rosé pétillant* for a fresh sensation). A dry rosé is popular in the Loire in the summer and can be made from a variety of grapes.

You'll pass vineyards as you travel between châteaux, though there's no scenic wine road to speak of (the closest thing is around Bourgueil). Remember that it's best to call ahead before visiting a winery.

East of Tours

Amboise

Straddling the widest stretch of the Loire River, Amboise is an inviting town with a fine old quarter below its hilltop château. A

castle has overlooked the Loire from Amboise since Roman times. Leonardo da Vinci retired here...just one more of his many brilliant ideas.

As the royal residence of François I (r. 1515-1547), Amboise wielded far more importance than you'd imagine from a lazy walk through its

pleasant, pedestrian-only commercial zone. In fact, its residents are quite conservative, giving the town an attitude—as if no one told them they're no longer the second capital of France. The locals keep their wealth to themselves; consequently, many grand mansions hide behind nondescript facades.

The half-mile-long "Golden Island" is the only island in the Loire substantial enough to be flood-proof and to have permanent buildings (including a soccer stadium and a 13th-century church). It was important historically as the place where northern and southern France, divided by the longest river in the country, came together. Truces were made here. The Loire marked the farthest point north that the Moors conquered as they pushed through

Europe from Morocco. (Loire means "impassable" in Arabic.) Today, this region still divides the country—for example, weather forecasters say, "north of the Loire...and south of the Loire..."

With or without a car, Amboise is an ideal small-town home base for exploring the best of château country.

Orientation to Amboise

Amboise (pop. 14,000) covers ground on both sides of the Loire, with the "Golden Island" (Ile d'Or) in the middle. The train station is on the north side of the Loire, but nearly everything else is on the south (château) side, including the TI and steady traffic. Pedestrian-friendly rue Nationale parallels the river a few blocks inland and leads from the base of Château d'Amboise through the town center and past the clock tower—once part of the town wall—to the striking Romanesque Church of St. Denis.

Tourist Information

The information-packed TI is on quai du Général de Gaulle (May-Sept Mon-Sat 9:30-18:30, Sun 9:30-13:00 & 14:00-17:00; Oct-April Mon-Sat 10:00-13:00 & 14:00-18:00, Sun 10:00-13:00; tel. 02 47 57 09 28, www.amboise-valdeloire.com). Pick up the brochures with self-guided walking tours in and around the city, and consider pre-purchasing tickets to key area châteaux (saving time in ticket lines—explained under "Helpful Hints," later). Ask about sound-and-light shows in the region (generally summers only). The TI stores bags (€2.50 each), books local guides, and can reserve a room for you in a hotel or *chambre d'hôte* (for a €2.50 fee)—but first peruse the photo album of regional *chambres d'hôtes*. Their free English-speaking service, SOS Chambres d'Hôtes, can tell you which rooms are still available when the TI is closed (tel. 02 47 23 27 42).

Arrival in Amboise

By Train: Amboise's train station is birds-chirping peaceful. You can't store bags here, but you can leave them at the TI (see above). Turn left out of the main station (you may have to cross under the tracks first), make a quick right, and walk down rue Jules Ferry five minutes to the end, then turn right and cross the long bridge leading over the Loire River to the city center. It's a €6 taxi ride from the station to central Amboise, but taxis seldom wait at the station (taxi tel. 02 47 57 13 53 or 02 47 57 30 39).

By Car: Drivers set their sights on the flag-festooned château that caps the hill. Most recommended accommodations and restaurants either have or can help you locate free parking.

THE LOIRE

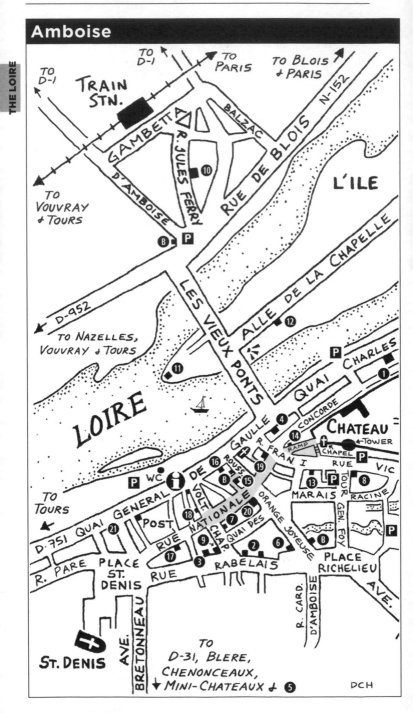

Amboise

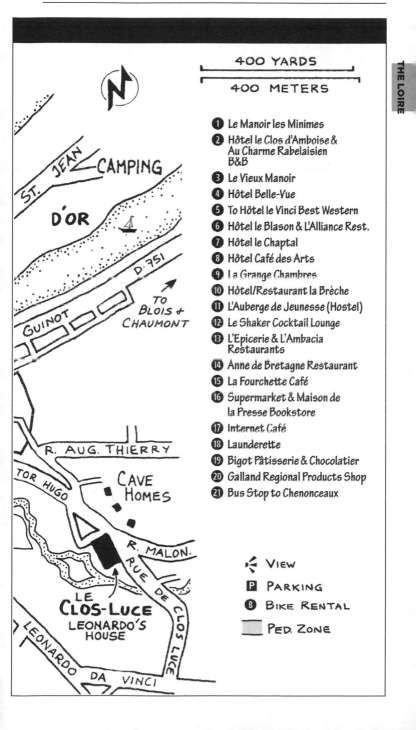

400 YARDS

400 METERS

1 Le Manoir les Minimes
2 Hôtel le Clos d'Amboise & Au Charme Rabelaisien B&B
3 Le Vieux Manoir
4 Hôtel Belle-Vue
5 To Hôtel le Vinci Best Western
6 Hôtel le Blason & L'Alliance Rest.
7 Hôtel le Chaptal
8 Hôtel Café des Arts
9 La Grange Chambres
10 Hôtel/Restaurant la Brèche
11 L'Auberge de Jeunesse (Hostel)
12 Le Shaker Cocktail Lounge
13 L'Epicerie & L'Ambacia Restaurants
14 Anne de Bretagne Restaurant
15 La Fourchette Café
16 Supermarket & Maison de la Presse Bookstore
17 Internet Café
18 Launderette
19 Bigot Pâtisserie & Chocolatier
20 Galland Regional Products Shop
21 Bus Stop to Chenonceaux

VIEW
P PARKING
B BIKE RENTAL
PED. ZONE

THE LOIRE

Helpful Hints

Save Time and Money: The TI sells tickets in bundles of three or four to sights and châteaux around Amboise and Chinon (called "le Pass", valid for a year). This will save you some on entry fees—and, more important, time spent in line at each sight (for example, the pass for Clos-Lucé and the châteaux of Amboise, Chambord, and Chaumont saves €5 over individual ticket prices). You can also get cheaper tickets if you take a minivan tour.

Market Days: Open-air markets are held on Friday (smaller but more local; food only) and Sunday (the big one) in the parking lot behind the TI on the river (both 8:30-13:00).

Regional Products: Galland, at 29 rue Nationale, sells fine food and wine products from the Loire (daily 9:30-19:00).

Supermarket: Carrefour City is near the TI (Mon-Sat 7:00-21:00, Sun 9:00-13:00), though the shops on pedestrian-only rue Nationale are infinitely more pleasing.

Internet Access: Playconnect Cyber C@fe has good rates and long hours (119 rue Nationale, tel. 02 47 57 18 04, www.play connect-cyber.com).

Bookstore: Maison de la Presse is a good bookstore with a small selection of English novels and a big selection of maps and English guidebooks—such as Michelin's Green Guide *Châteaux of the Loire* (English version costs €16; bookstore open Mon 14:00-19:00, Tue-Sat 8:00-19:00, Sun 9:00-13:00, across from the TI at 5 quai du Général de Gaulle).

Laundry: The handy coin-op **Lav'centre** is near the TI, up allée du Sergent Turpin at #9 (allow €7/load, daily 7:00-20:00, last wash at 19:00, English instructions). The door locks at closing time; leave beforehand, or you'll trigger the alarm.

Bike Rental: You can rent a bike (€11/half-day, €14/day, leave your passport or a photocopy) at either of these reliable places: **Locacycle** (daily 9:00-12:30 & 14:00-19:00, full-day rentals can be returned the next morning, 2 rue Jean-Jacques Rousseau, tel. 02 47 57 00 28) or **Cycles le Duc** (good bikes, Tue-Sat 9:00-12:00 & 14:30-19:00, closed Sun-Mon, 5 rue Joyeuse, tel. 02 47 57 00 17). The signed bike route to Chenonceaux leads past Leonardo's Clos-Lucé.

Taxi: Call 02 47 57 13 53 or 02 47 57 30 39 (allow €25 to Chenonceaux, €35 in the evening or on Sun).

Car Rental: You can rent cars at the St. Pierre-des-Corps train station (TGV service from Paris), a 15-minute drive from Amboise. On the outskirts of Amboise, **Garage Jourdain** rents cars (roughly €48/day for a small car with 100 kilometers/62 miles free, Mon-Fri 7:45-12:00 & 14:00-18:00, Sat 9:00-12:00 & 14:00-17:00, closed Sun, about a mile downriver from the TI at 105 avenue de Tours, tel. 02 47 57 17 92, fax 02 47 57 77 50). Pricier **Europcar** is outside Amboise on route de Chenonceaux at the Total gas station (about €65/day for a small car, tel. 02 47 57 07 64, fax 02 47 23 25 14, www.europcar .com). Figure €7 for a taxi from Amboise to either place.

Chocolate Fantasy: A tasty and historic stop for chocoholics is **Bigot Pâtisserie & Chocolatier.** Try their specialty, Puits d'Amour—"Well of Love" (daily, one block off the river, where place Michel Debré meets rue Nationale, tel. 02 47 57 04 46).

Private Guide: Fabrice Maret lives in Blois but is an expert in all things Loire and a great teacher. He can meet you in Amboise to give an excellent walking tour of the city and its sights, or join your car and guide you around the area's châteaux (€260/ day plus transportation from Blois, tel. 02 54 70 19 59, www .chateauxloire.com, info@chateauxloire.com).

Wine-Tasting: At **Loire Uncorked,** British expats Tom and Amanda Humphreys offer small, informal wine-tasting tours for up to six people. Wanting to dispel the myth that tasting is only for connoisseurs, they'll show you the great variety of wines from their adopted region (€155/person for a full day of tastings and restaurant lunch, €195 Gourmet Tour has a fancier lunch, British tel. 01672/519-038, from France dial 00-44-1672-519-038, www.loireuncorked.com).

Self-Guided Walk

Welcome to Amboise

This short walk starts at the banks of the Loire River, winds past the old church of St. Denis, and meanders through the heart of town to a fine little city museum. You'll end near the entrance to Château Royal d'Amboise and Leonardo's house.

• *Climb to the top of the embankment overlooking the river (anywhere downstream from the bridge works).*

Amboise Riverbank: Survey the town, its island, bridge, and castle. If you have a passion for anything French—philosophy, history, food, wine—you'll feel it here, along the Loire. This river, the longest in France and the natural boundary between northern and southern France, is the last "untamed" river in the country (there are no dams or mechanisms to control periodic flooding). The region's châteaux line up along the Loire and its tributaries, because before trains and trucks, stones for big buildings were best shipped by boat. You may see a few of the traditional flat-bottomed Loire boats moored here. The bridge spanning the river isn't just any bridge. It marks a strategic river crossing and a longtime political border. That's why the first Amboise castle was built here. In the 15th century, this was one of the biggest forts in France.

• *With your back to the river, head away from the water and veer right along quai du Général de Gaulle. Looking to your left, head toward the old church standing proudly on a bluff (see map).*

Church of St. Denis (Eglise St. Denis): Ever since ancient Romans erected a Temple of Mars here, this has been a place of worship. According to legend, God sent a bolt of lightning that knocked down the statue of Mars, and Christians took over the spot. The current Romanesque church dates from the 12th century. A cute little statue of St. Denis (above the round arch) greets you as you step in. The delightful carvings capping the columns inside date from Romanesque times. The lovely pastel-painted *Deposition* is restored to its 16th-century brilliance. The medieval stained glass in the windows, likely destroyed in the French Revolution, was replaced with 19th-century glass.

From the steps of the church, look out to the hill-capping Amboise château. For a thousand years, it's been God on this hill and the king on that one. It's interesting to ponder how, throughout French history, the king's power generally trumped the Church's, and how the Church and the king worked to keep people down—setting the stage for the French Revolution.

• *From place St. Denis in front of the church, follow rue Nationale through the heart of town in the direction of the castle.*

Rue Nationale: In France, districts around any castle or church officially classified as historic are preserved. The broad, pedestrianized rue Nationale, with its narrow intersecting lanes, survives from the 15th century. At that time, when the town spread at the foot of the king's castle, this was the "Champs-Elysées" of Amboise. Supporting the king and his huge entourage was a serious industry. The French king spilled money wherever he stayed.

As you walk along this spine of the town, spot surviving bits of rustic medieval oak in the half-timbered buildings. The homes of wealthy merchants rose from the chaos of this street. Side lanes can be more candid—they often show what's hidden behind modern facades.

Pass through the impressive clock tower *(porte de l'horloge)*, built into part of the town wall that dates back to the 15th century. This was once a fortified gate, opening onto the road to the city of Tours. Imagine the hefty wood-and-iron portcullis (fortified door) that dropped from above.

• *At the intersection with rue François I (where you'll be tempted by the Bigot chocolate shop—see "Helpful Hints," earlier), turn left a couple of steps to the...*

City Hall Museum (Musée de Hôtel de Ville): This free

museum is worth a quick peek for its romantic interior, town paintings, and historic etchings (mid-June-mid-Sept Wed-Mon 10:00-12:30 & 14:00-18:00, closed Tue and off-season). Upstairs, in the still-functioning city assembly hall, notice how the photo of the current president faces the lady of the Republic. (According to locals, her features change with the taste of the generation, and the bust of France's Lady Liberty is often modeled on famous super-models of the day.)

• *Your walk ends here, but you can easily continue on to the nearby Château Royal d'Amboise (and beyond that, to Leonardo's last residence): Retrace your steps along rue François I to place Michel Debré, at the base of the château. Here, at one of the most touristy spots in the Loire, you can feel how important tourism is to the local economy. Notice the fat, round 15th-century fortified tower, whose interior ramp was built for galloping horses to spiral up to castle level. But to get to the castle without a horse, you'll have to walk the ramp to the left.*

Sights In Amboise

▲Château Royal d'Amboise

This historic heap became the favored royal residence in the Loire under Charles VIII, who did most of the building in the late 15th

century. Charles is famous for accidentally killing himself by walking into a door lintel on his way to a tennis match (seriously). Later occupants include Louis XII (who moved the royal court to Blois) and François I (who physically brought the Renaissance here in 1516, in the person of Leonardo da Vinci).

Cost and Hours: €10 plus €3.50 for audioguide (kid's version available), daily April-June 9:00-18:30, July-Aug 9:00-19:00, Sept-Oct and March 9:00-18:00, Nov-Jan 9:00-12:00 & 14:00-16:45, Feb 9:00-12:00 & 13:30-17:30, place Michel Debré, tel. 02 47 57 00 98, www.chateau-amboise.com.

Touring the Château: After climbing the long ramp to the ticket booth and picking up the good English handout, our first stop is the petite **chapel** where Leonardo da Vinci is supposedly buried. This flamboyant little Gothic chapel comes with two fire-places "to comfort the king" and two plaques "evoking the final resting place" of Leonardo (one in French, the other in Italian). Where he's actually buried, no one seems to know. Look up at the ceiling to appreciate the lacy design.

The **gardens** come with grand river and château views. Each summer, bleachers are set up for sound-and-light spectacles—a faint echo of the extravaganzas Leonardo orchestrated for the court. Modern art decorating the garden reminds visitors of the inquisitive and scientific Renaissance spirit that Leonardo brought to town. The flags are those of France and Brittany—a reminder that, in a sense, modern France was created at the nearby château of Langeais when Charles VIII (who was born here) married Anne of Brittany, adding her domain to the French kingdom.

Wandering through the **castle rooms,** the route takes you chronologically from Gothic-style rooms to those from the early Renaissance and on to the 19th century. In the Salle des Gardes, plans show the château's original, much larger size. Some wings added in the 15th and 16th centuries have disappeared. (The little chapel you just saw was once part of the bigger complex.) The rose-colored top-floor rooms are well-furnished from the post-Revolutionary 1800s and demonstrate the continued interest in this château among French nobility.

Climb to the top of the **Minimes Tower** for grand views. From here, the strategic value of this site is clear: The visibility is great, and the river below provided a natural defense. The bulky tower climbs 130 feet in five spirals—designed for a mounted soldier in a hurry.

There are two exits. While you can leave the way you came, it's more interesting to spiral down the **Heurtault Tower** (access through the gift shop near the top of the entry ramp). As with the castle's other tower, this was designed to accommodate a soldier on horseback. As you gallop down to the exit, notice the cute little characters and scenes left by 15th-century stone-carvers. While they needed to behave when decorating churches and palaces, here they could be a bit racier and more spirited.

Leaving the Château: The turnstile puts you on the road to Château du Clos-Lucé (described next; turn left and hike straight for 10 minutes). Along the way, you'll pass **troglodyte houses**—both new and old—carved into the hillside. Originally, poor people resided here—the dwellings didn't require expensive slate roofing, came with natural insulation, and could be dug essentially for free, as builders valued the stone quarried in the process. Today wealthy stone-lovers are renovating them into stylish digs worthy of *Better Homes and Caves*. You can see chimneys high above. Unfortunately, none are open to the public.

▲Château du Clos-Lucé and Leonardo da Vinci Park

In 1516, Leonardo da Vinci packed his bags (and several of his favorite paintings, including the *Mona Lisa*) and left an imploding Rome for better wine and working conditions in the Loire Valley. He accepted the position of engineer, architect, and painter

to France's Renaissance king, François I. This "House of Light" is the plush palace where Leonardo spent his last three years. (He died on May 2, 1519.) François, only 22 years old, installed the 65-year-old Leonardo here just so he could enjoy his intellectual company.

The house is a kind of fort-château of its own, with a fortified rampart walk and a 16th-century chapel. While the present owners keep the upstairs to themselves, an entire floor of finely decorated and furnished rooms is open to the public.

Leonardo came with disciples, who also stayed active here, using this house as a kind of workshop and laboratory. The place survived the Revolution because the quick-talking noble who owned it was sympathetic to the cause; he convinced the Revolutionaries that philosophically, Leonardo would have been on their side.

Cost and Hours: The €13 admission, while pricey, is worth it for Leonardo fans with two hours to spend taking full advantage of this sight. Daily April-Oct 9:00-19:00, Nov-Dec and Feb-March 9:00-18:00, Jan 9:00-17:00, follow the helpful free English handout, tel. 02 47 57 00 73, www.vinci-closluce.com.

Cuisine Art: The garden café is reasonably priced and appropriately meditative. For a view over Amboise, choose the terrace *crêperie.*

Getting There: It's a 10-minute walk uphill from Château Royal d'Amboise, past troglodyte homes (see end of previous listing). If you drive, note that the parking lot near Clos-Lucé is unsafe—don't leave valuables visible in your car.

Touring the Château and Gardens: Your visit begins with a tour of Leonardo's elegant yet livable Renaissance **home.** This little residence was built in 1450—just within the protective walls of the town—as a guesthouse for the king's château nearby. Today it thoughtfully re-creates (with Renaissance music) the everyday atmosphere Leonardo enjoyed while he lived here, pursuing his passions to the very end. Find the touching sketch in Leonardo's bedroom of François I comforting his genius pal on his deathbed, and see copies of Leonardo's most famous paintings (including the *Mona Lisa*).

The basement level is filled with **sketches** recording the storm patterns of Leonardo's brain and **models** of his remarkable inventions (inspired by nature and built according to his notes). Leonardo was fascinated by water. All he lacked was steam power. It's hard to imagine that this Roman candle of creativity died nearly 500

THE LOIRE

The Loire and Its Many Châteaux:
A Historical Primer

It's hard to overstate the importance of the Loire River to France. Its place in French history goes back to the very foundation of the country. As if to proclaim its storied past, the Loire is the last major wild river in France, with no dams and no regulation of its flow.

Traditional flat-bottomed boats romantically moored along embankments are a reminder of the age before trains and trucks, when river traffic safely and efficiently transported heavy loads of stone and timber. With prevailing winds sweeping east from the Atlantic, barge tenders raised their sails and headed upriver; on the way back, boats flowed downstream with the current.

With this transportation infrastructure and the region's thick forests—providing plenty of timber, firewood, and hunting terrain—it's no wonder that castles were built here in the Middle Ages. The first stone fortresses went up here a thousand years ago, and many of the pleasure palaces you see today rose over the ruins of those original defensive keeps.

The Hundred Years' War—roughly 1336 to 1453—was a desperate time for France. Because of a dynastic dispute, the English had a serious claim to the French throne, and by 1415 they controlled much of the country, including Paris. France was at a low ebb, and its king and court retreated to the Loire Valley to rule what remained of their realm. Chinon was the refuge of the dispirited king, Charles VII. He was famously visited there in 1429 by the charismatic Joan of Arc, who inspired the king to get off his duff and send the English packing.

The French kings continued to live on the Loire for the next two centuries, having grown comfortable with the château culture of the region. The climate was mild, hunting was good, dreamy rivers made nice reflections, wealthy friends lived in similar luxury nearby, and the location was close enough to Paris—but still far enough away. Charles VII ruled from Chinon, Charles VIII preferred Amboise, Louis XII reigned from Blois, and François I held court in Chambord and Blois.

This was a kind of cultural Golden Age. With peace and stability, there was no need for fortifications. The most famous luxury hunting lodges, masquerading as fortresses, were built during this period—including Chenonceau, Chambord, Chaumont, Amboise, and Azay-le-Rideau. Kings (François I), writers (Rabelais), poets (Ronsard), and artists (Leonardo da Vinci) made the Loire a cultural hub.

Because French kings ruled effectively only by being constantly on the move, many royal châteaux were used infrequently. The entire court—and its trappings—had to be portable. A castle kept empty and cold eleven months of the year would suddenly become the busy center of attention when the king came to town. As you visit the castles, imagine the royal roadies setting up a kingly room—hanging tapestries, unfolding chairs, wrestling big trunks with handles—in the hours just before the arrival of the royal entourage. The French word for furniture, *mobilier,* literally means "mobile."

When touring the châteaux, you'll notice the impact of Italian culture. From the Renaissance onward, Italian ways were fancy ways. French nobles and court ministers who traveled to Italy returned inspired by the art and architecture they saw. Kings imported Italian artists and architects. It's no wonder that the ultimate French Renaissance king, François I, invited the ultimate Italian artist, Leonardo da Vinci, to join his court in Amboise. Tastes in food, gardens, artists, and women were all influenced by Italian culture.

And women had a big impact on Loire château life. Big personalities like kings tickled more than one tiara. Louis XV famously decorated the palace of Chenonceau with a painting of the Three Graces—featuring his three favorite mistresses.

Châteaux were generally owned by kings, their ministers, or their mistresses. A high-maintenance and powerful mistress often managed to get her own place even when a king's romantic interest shifted elsewhere. In many cases, the king or minister would be away on work or at war for years at a time—leaving home-improvement decisions to the lady of the château, who had unlimited money. That helps explain the emphasis on comfort and the feminine touch you'll enjoy while touring many of the Loire châteaux.

In 1525, François I moved to his newly built super-palace at Fontainebleau, and political power left the Loire. From then on, châteaux were mostly used as vacation and hunting retreats. They become refuges for kings again during the French Wars of Religion (1562-1598)—a sticky set of squabbles over dynastic control that pitted Protestants (Huguenots) against Catholics. Its conclusion marked the end of an active royal presence on the Loire. With the French Revolution in 1789, symbols of the Old Regime, like the fabulous palaces along the Loire, were ransacked. Fast talking saved some châteaux, especially those whose owners had personal relationships with Revolutionary leaders.

Only in the 1840s did the châteaux of the Loire become appreciated for their historic value. The Loire was the first place where treasures of French heritage were officially recognized and protected by the national government. In the 19th century, Romantic Age writers—like Victor Hugo and Alexander Dumas—visited and celebrated the châteaux. Aristocrats on the Grand Tour stopped here. The Loire Valley and its historic châteaux found a place in our collective hearts and have been treasured to this day.

years ago. Imagine Leonardo's résumé letter to kings of Europe: "I can help your armies by designing tanks, flying machines, wind-up cars, gear systems, extension ladders, and water pumps." The French considered him a futurist who never really implemented his visions.

Your visit finishes with a stroll through the whimsical and very kid-friendly **park grounds,** with life-size models of Leonardo's inventions (including some that function, such as a "revolving bridge"), "sound stations" (in English), and translucent replicas of some of his paintings. The models make clear that much of what Leonardo observed and created was based on his intense study of nature.

Other Sights

▲Château Royal d'Amboise Sound-and-Light Show—If you're into S&L, this is considered one of the best shows of its kind in the area. Although it's entirely in French, you can buy the English booklet for €5. Volunteer locals from toddlers to pensioners re-create the life of François I with costumes, juggling, impressive light displays, and fireworks. Dress warmly.

Cost and Hours: €17, family deals, only about 20 performances a year, 1.5-hour show, Wed and Sat late June-July 22:30-24:00, Aug 22:00-23:30, tel. 02 47 57 14 47, www.renaissance-amboise.com. The ticket window is on the ramp to the château and opens at 20:30.

Mini-Châteaux—This scruffy five-acre park on the edge of Amboise (on the route to Chenonceaux) shows the major Loire châteaux in 1:25-scale models, forested with 2,000 bonsai trees and laced together by a model TGV train and river boats. For children, it's a fun introduction to the real châteaux they'll be visiting (and a cool toy store). Essential English information is posted throughout the sight.

You'll find other kid-oriented attractions at Mini-Châteaux; consider playing a round of mini-golf and feeding the fish in the moat (a great way to get rid of that old baguette).

Cost and Hours: Adults-€14, kids-€10, daily June-Aug 10:00-20:00, Sept-Oct 10:30-18:00, April-May 10:30-19:00, closed Nov-March, last entry one hour before closing, tel. 02 47 23 44 57, www.mini-chateaux.com.

Caveau des Vignerons—This small *cave* offers free tastings of cheeses, patés, and regional wines from 10 different vintners.

Cost and Hours: Free tasting room, mid-March-mid-Nov daily 10:00-19:00, under Château d'Amboise, across from recommended l'Epicerie restaurant, tel. 02 47 57 23 69.

Biking from Amboise—Allow an hour to Chenonceaux (about 8 miles one-way). The first two miles are uphill, and the entire ride is on a road with light traffic. White-and-green biking signs will guide you past Clos-Lucé to Chenonceaux. Serious cyclists can continue to Chaumont in 1.5 hours, connecting Amboise, Chenonceaux, and Chaumont in an all-day, 37-mile pedal (see "Recommended Bike Route" on the map on page 34).

Canoe Trips from Amboise or Chenonceaux—Paddling under the Château de Chenonceau is a memorable experience. **Canoe Company** offers canoe rentals on the Loire and Cher rivers (€12-22/person depending on how far you go, tel. 06 70 13 30 61, www.canoe-company.fr).

Near Amboise

Wine-Tasting in Vouvray—In the nearby town of Vouvray, 10 miles toward Tours from Amboise, you'll find wall-to-wall opportunities for wine-tasting, including a convenient, top-quality winery, **Marc Brédif**. They have a good if pricey selection of Vouvray wines, as well as red wines from Chinon and Bourgueil (the most reputed reds in the Loire). Reserve ahead for their wine-and-cheese-tastings, where five wines are paired with different cheeses. You can also take a €5 tour of their impressive 1.2 miles of cellars dug into the hillside.

    Cost and Hours: Free tasting room, Mon-Fri 9:00-12:00 & 14:00-18:00, Sat 10:30-12:00 & 13:00-18:00, Sun 10:30-13:00, tel. 02 47 52 50 07.

    Getting There: Coming from Amboise, you'll pass it on D-952 after Vouvray in the direction of Tours; it's on the right, a few hundred yards after you enter Rochecorbon.

ZooParc de Beauval—If you need a zoo fix, this is France's biggest and most impressive one, with thousands of animals from the land and sea. It's about 30 minutes southeast of Amboise toward Vierzon—pick up details at the TI.

    Cost and Hours: Adults-€22, kids 3-10-€16, daily from 9:00 to dusk, tel. 02 54 75 50 00, www.zoobeauval.com.

Sleeping in Amboise

Amboise is busy in the summer, but there are lots of reasonable hotels and *chambres d'hôtes* in and around the city; the TI can help with reservations (for a €2.50 fee).

In the Town Center

$$$ Le Manoir les Minimes**** is a good place to experience the refined air of château life in a 17th-century mansion, with antique furniture and precious art objects in the public spaces. Its 15 large, modern rooms work for those seeking luxury digs in Amboise (tall

THE LOIRE

Sleep Code

(€1 = about $1.40, country code: 33)
S = Single, **D** = Double/Twin, **T** = Triple, **Q** = Quad, **b** = bathroom, **s** = shower only, ***** = French hotel rating system (0-5 stars). Unless otherwise noted, credit cards are accepted and English is spoken.

To help you easily sort through these listings, I've divided the accommodations into three categories based on the price for a standard double room with bath:

$$$ Higher Priced—Most rooms €90 or more.
 $$ Moderately Priced—Most rooms between €60-90.
  $ Lower Priced—Most rooms €60 or less.

Prices can change without notice; verify the hotel's current rates online or by email. For other updates, see www.ricksteves.com/update.

folks take note: top-floor attic rooms have low ceilings). Several rooms have views of Amboise's château (standard Db-€129-145, larger Db-€175-200, suite-€290, 3- to 4-person suites-€490, extra bed-€27, air-con, Wi-Fi, three blocks upriver from bridge at 34 quai Charles Guinot, tel. 02 47 30 40 40, fax 02 47 30 40 77, www.manoirlesminimes.com, reservation@manoirlesminimes.com, helpful Patrice and Eric).

$$$ Hôtel le Clos d'Amboise*** is a top upscale value. This smart urban refuge opens onto beautiful gardens and a small pool, offering stay-awhile lounges and well-designed rooms that mix a touch of modern with a classic, traditional look (standard Db-€95, bigger Db-€150-180, Db suites-€210-310, extra person-€20, elevator, small fridges, good buffet breakfast-€12, air-con, Wi-Fi, sauna, free parking, 27 rue Rabelais, tel. 02 47 30 10 20, fax 02 47 57 33 43, www.leclosamboise.com, info@leclosamboise.com, helpful Patricia or Guillaume are ever-present).

$$$ Le Vieux Manoir*** is an entirely different high-end splurge. American expats Gloria and Bob Belknap have restored this secluded but central onetime convent with an attention to detail that Martha Stewart could learn from. The gardens are lovely, as are the atrium-like breakfast room, sitting lounge, and six bedrooms that would make an antique collector drool. Eager-to-help Gloria

is a one-person tourist office (Db-€160-185, cottages-€240-300 and require 3-night minimum stay, includes superb breakfast, non-smoking, air-con, Internet access and Wi-Fi in lobby, no room phones or TVs, free parking, 13 rue Rabelais, tel. & fax 02 47 30 41 27, www.le-vieux-manoir.com, le_vieux_manoir@yahoo.com).

$$ Hôtel Belle-Vue** is a centrally located and traditional place overlooking the river where the bridge hits the town. Closed in 2011 for renovation, the hotel will reopen in 2012, likely with higher rates (Db-€68-78, Tb-€88, two-room Tb-€98, two-room Qb-€125, elevator, Wi-Fi in lobby, 12 quai Charles Guinot, tel. 02 47 57 02 26, fax 02 47 30 51 23, www.hotel-bellevue-amboise.com, contact@hotel-bellevue-amboise.com).

$$ Hôtel le Vinci Best Western** is well-run and modern, providing good midrange comfort a mile from the town center toward Chenonceaux. Meals are possible on the back terrace (standard Db-€82-92, superior Db-€102, extra person-€20, 12 avenue Emile Gounin, tel. 02 47 57 10 90, fax 02 47 57 17 52, www.vinci loirevalley.com, reservation@vinciloirevalley.com).

$ Hôtel le Blason**, in a 15th-century, half-timbered building five blocks from the river on a busy street, is run by helpful Damien and Beranger, who speak English. The rooms—some with ship's-cabin-like bathrooms—are tight and bright, and have double-paned windows. There's air-conditioning on the top floor (Sb-€50, Db-€60, Tb-€70, Qb-€80, quieter rooms in back and on top floor, free Internet access and Wi-Fi, secure parking-€3, 11 place Richelieu, tel. 02 47 23 22 41, fax 02 47 57 56 18, www.le blason.fr, hotel@leblason.fr).

$ Hotel le Chaptal** is a plain, modern hotel with small but clean and cheap rooms (Db-€50-55, Tb-€68, Qb-€80, Wi-Fi, 11 rue Chaptal, tel. 02 47 57 14 46, fax 02 47 57 67 83, www.hotel -chaptal-amboise.fr, infos@hotel-chaptal-amboise.fr).

$ Café des Arts feels more like a hostel, with seven spartan but clean, bright, and bunky rooms lodged above a local bar/café next to the château (S-€34, D-€44, T-€65, Qb-€70, 32 rue Victor Hugo, tel. & fax 02 47 57 25 04, www.cafedesarts.net, cafedesarts .amboise@sfr.fr).

Chambres d'Hôtes

The heart of Amboise offers several solid bed-and-breakfast options.

$$$ Au Charme Rabelaisien is a drop-dead-gorgeous place run by drop-dead-charming Madame Viard. Big doors from the street open onto a grand courtyard with manicured gardens, a heated pool, and three sumptuous rooms surrounding it (small Db-€92, roomy Db-€135-170, €20 for third person—child only, includes breakfast, air-con, Wi-Fi, private parking, 25 rue

Rabelais, tel. 02 47 57 53 84, fax 02 22 44 19 24, www.au-charme
-rabelaisien.com, aucharmerabelaisien@wanadoo.fr).

$$ La Grange Chambres welcomes with an intimate, flow-
ery courtyard. Each of the four comfortable rooms has been taste-
fully restored with modern conveniences and big beds. There's also
a common room with a fridge and tables for do-it-yourself din-
ners (Db-€78-85, extra person-€20, includes breakfast, cash only,
where rues Châptal and Rabelais meet at 18 rue Châptal, tel. 02 47
57 57 22, www.la-grange-amboise.com, info@la-grange-amboise
.com). Adorable Yveline Savin also rents a small two-room cottage
(€440-560/week, 2- to 3-day stays possible).

Near the Train Station
$$ Hôtel la Brèche*, a sleepy place near the station, has 14
excellent-value rooms and a good restaurant. Many rooms overlook
the peaceful graveled garden, while those on the street are generally
larger and come with some traffic noise; all are tastefully decorated
(Sb-€52, Db-€55-65, Tb-€74, Qb-€90, room for up to six-€95,
breakfast-€7, Wi-Fi, 15-minute walk from city center and 2-minute
walk from station, 26 rue Jules Ferry, tel. 02 47 57 00 79, fax 02
47 57 65 49, www.labreche-amboise.com, info@labreche-amboise
.com).

Hostel: **$ L'Auberge de Jeunesse** (Centre Charles Péguy)
is ideally located on the western tip of the "Golden Island," a
10-minute walk from the train station. Open to people of all ages,
and popular with student groups, it's friendly and easy on the wallet.
There are a handful of double rooms—some with partial views to
the château—so book ahead (D-€26, bunk in 3- to 4-bed room-
€13, sheets-€3, no surcharge for nonmembers, breakfast-€4.50,
dinner-€10, reception open daily 15:00-20:00, no curfew, Ile d'Or,
tel. 02 47 30 60 90, fax 02 47 30 60 91, www.mjcamboise.fr, cis
@mjcamboise.fr).

Sleeping near Amboise

The area around Amboise is replete with good-value accommodations of every shape, size, and price range. This region offers drivers
the best chance to experience château life at affordable rates—and
my recommendations justify the detour. Also consider the recommended accommodations in Chenonceaux and the Hôtel du
Grand St. Michel at Chambord.

$$$ Château de Pray**** is a 750-year-old fortified castle
with hints of its medieval origins. The 14 rooms in the main châ-
teau come with appropriately heavy furniture, lots of character,
and tubs in most bathrooms. A newer annex offers four contem-

porary rooms (sleeping up to three each), with lofts, terraces, and views of the castle. An overflowing pool and the restaurant's vegetable garden lie below the château (small Db in main building-€150-200, Db in annex-€145, family room-€250, extra bed-€40, breakfast-€15, no air-con, 3-minute drive upriver from Amboise toward Chaumont on D-751, tel. 02 47 57 23 67, fax 02 47 57 32 50, http://praycastel.online.fr, praycastel@online.fr). The dining room is splendid and a relaxing place to splurge and feel good about it (four-course *menus* from €53, reservations required).

$$$ Château des Ormeaux Chambres d'Hôte is run by attentive owners—Eric, Emmanuel, and Dominique—who rent five wonderfully traditional rooms with huge bathrooms in a lovingly restored 18th-century château. The place has a pool and a grand terrace overlooking the forest (Db-€120-170, includes breakfast, Wi-Fi in lobby, across the river from Amboise in Nazelles, Route de Noizay, tel. 02 47 23 26 51, fax 02 47 23 19 31, www.chateaudesormeaux.fr, contact@chateaudesormeaux.fr). From D-952, take D-5 into Nazelles-Négron, turn left on D-1, and find it on the right after a few miles.

$$$ At Château de Nazelles Chambres, gentle owners Veronique and Olivier Fructus offer five rooms in a 16th-century hillside manor house that was once home to Chenonceau's original builder. It comes with a cliff-sculpted pool, manicured gardens, a guest's kitchen (picnics are encouraged), views over Amboise, trails to the forest above, and a classy living room with billiards, computer access, and Wi-Fi. The two bedrooms in the main building are just grand, while the rooms cut into the rock come with private grass terraces and rock-walled bathrooms (Db-€110, bigger Db-€145, includes breakfast, tel. & fax 02 47 30 53 79, www.chateau-nazelles.com, info@chateau-nazelles.com). From D-952, take D-5 into Nazelles-Négron, then turn left on D-1 and quickly veer right above the post office (PTT) to 16 rue Tue-la-Soif. Look for the sign on your left, and enter through the archway on the right.

$$$ Château des Arpentis*,** a medieval château-hotel centrally located just minutes from Amboise, makes a fun and classy splurge. Flanked by woods and acres of grass, and fronted by a stream and a moat, you'll come as close as you can to château life during the Loire's Golden Age. Rooms are big, with tasteful decor—and the pool is even bigger (Db-€130-185, amazing family suites-€220-370, air-con, Wi-Fi, near St. Règle, tel. 02 47 23 00 00, fax 02 47 52 62 17, www.chateaudesarpentis.com, contact@chateau desarpentis.com). It's on D-31 just southeast of Amboise; from the roundabout above the Leclerc Market, follow *Autrèche* signs, then look for the lane on the right marked by a tall flag.

$$ L'Auberge de Launay, five miles upriver from Amboise, gets rave reviews for its easy driving access to many châteaux, its warm welcome, and its wonderful restaurant. Owners François and Hélène are natural hosts at this comfortable 15-room hotel and restaurant (roadside Db-€66, bigger garden-side Db-€76, Wi-Fi; about 4 miles from Amboise, across the river toward Blois, at 9 rue de la Rivière in Limeray; tel. 02 47 30 16 82, www.aubergede launay.com, info@aubergedelaunay.com). The star of this place is the country-classy restaurant, with *menus* from €26 (closed Sun).

$ La Chevalerie owner Martine Aleksic rents four simple bargain *chambres* that are family-friendly in every way. You'll get a warm reception and total seclusion in a farm setting, with a swing set, tiny fishing pond, shared kitchens, and connecting rooms (Sb-€40, Db-€50, Tb-€60, Qb-€76, includes breakfast with fresh eggs, cash only, in La Croix-en-Touraine, tel. 02 47 57 83 64, lyoubisa .aleksic@orange.fr). From Amboise, take D-31 toward Bléré, look for the *Chambres d'Hôte* sign on your left at about three miles, and then turn left onto C-105.

$$ Le Moulin du Fief Gentil is a lovely 16th-century mill house set on four acres. Amenities include a backyard pond (fishing possible in summer, dinner picnics anytime, fridge and microwave at your disposal), the possibility of home-cooked dinners by English-speaking owner Fleurance (four-course dinner *menu* with wine-€30), and large, well-designed rooms (twin Db-€84, bigger Db-€100-120, 2-room apartment-€140, extra person-€22, includes breakfast, cash only, tel. 02 47 30 32 51, mobile 06 64 82 37 18, www .fiefgentil.com, contact@fiefgentil.com). It's located on the edge of Bléré, a 15-minute drive from Amboise and Chenonceaux—from Bléré, follow signs toward *Luzille*, and it's on the right.

$$ Hostellerie du Château de L'Isle is a rustic, lost-in-time place wrapped in a lush park on the Cher River with a pond and acres of grass. Located in Civray-de-Touraine, 15 minutes south of Amboise and two minutes from Chenonceaux, it offers 12 sufficiently comfortable rooms with laissez-faire management. Rooms in the main building are better (small Db-€55, standard Db-€70, big Db-€85-105, tel. 02 47 23 63 60, www.chateau-de-lisle.com, chateaudelisle@wanadoo.fr). The gazebo-like restaurant, as lovely as a Monet painting, features the owner's cooking (€26-36 meals, limited choices). From the center of Civray-de-Touraine, follow D-81 toward Tours.

Eating in Amboise

Amboise is filled with inexpensive and forgettable restaurants, but a handful of places are worth your attention. Many local eateries offer a good, end-of-meal cheese platter—a rarity in France these days. The epicenter of the city's dining action is on place Michel Debré, along rue Victor Hugo, and across from the château entrance. After dinner, make sure to cross the bridge for floodlit views of the castle, and consider a view drink at **Le Shaker Cocktail Lounge** (daily from 18:00 until later than you're awake, 3 quai François Tissard).

Dining Below the Château

L'Epicerie, across from the château entry, serves delicious and well-presented traditional cuisine at fair prices. Choose a table outdoors facing the château or in the rustically elegant dining room. The snails are incredible, the sauces are delectable, and the service is attentive. The €26 and €34 *menus* come with an amazing cheese platter (good *menus* from €23, July-Sept daily, Oct-June closed Mon-Tue, reserve ahead, 46 place Michel Debré, tel. 02 47 57 08 94).

Anne de Bretagne is an appealing brasserie, offering classic-but-simple dishes (such as crudités, crêpes, omelets, and French onion soup) at good prices. The outdoor tables are perfect for surveying the street scene, and the indoor tables come with cozy decor (nonstop service daily 12:00-22:00, place du Château, tel. 02 47 57 05 46).

L'Ambacia, with tables spilling out on the broad sidewalk, is a trendy, casual bistro serving everything from bagels to gourmet hamburgers to pasta (€9-14 *plats,* 12 place Michel Debré, tel. 02 47 23 21 44).

Elsewhere in Amboise

L'Alliance is a handsome restaurant run by a young couple (Pamela and Ludovica) trying to make their mark in Amboise. You'll dine well on creatively prepared regional specialties in a calming outdoor "greenhouse" or inside with more formal decor. Service can be slow (*menus* from €22-40, closed Tue-Wed, next to Hôtel le Blason at 14 rue Joyeuse, tel. 02 47 30 52 13).

La Fourchette is Amboise's family diner, with simple decor inside and out. Chef Christine makes everything fresh in her open kitchen, offering a limited selection at good prices (€15-24 *menus,* closed Sun-Mon, on a quiet corner near rue Nationale at 9 rue Malebranche, tel. 06 11 78 16 98).

Hôtel la Brèche serves a good-value €20 *menu* in their warm, traditional dining room and large garden. Stretch your legs and cross the river to the restaurant, then enjoy floodlit castle views on your walk home (daily; for details, see "Sleeping in Amboise," earlier).

Near Amboise

These places merit the short drive. It's best to call ahead to reserve. For a royal experience, consider making the quick drive to **Château de Pray.** For a warm welcome and good cuisine, call to find out if Hélène can take you at **L'Auberge de Launay.** For vintage French cuisine, head for **Auberge du Cheval Rouge** near Chenonceaux. To add a Michelin star to your portfolio, aim for Chenonceaux and the **Auberge du Bon Laboureur.**

Amboise Connections

By Bus and Taxi

From Amboise to Nearby Châteaux: For easiest access to area châteaux, see "Getting Around the Loire Valley" on page 5.

By Bus to: Chenonceaux (1-2/day, Mon-Sat only, none on Sun, 20 minutes, one-way-€1.10; departs Amboise about 9:45, returns from Chenonceaux at about 12:15, allowing you about an hour and 20 minutes at the château; in summer, there's also an afternoon departure at about 15:00, with a return from Chenonceaux at about 17:20; the Amboise stop—called Théâtre—is between place St. Denis and the river on the west side of avenue des Martyrs de la Résistance, confirm times with the TI; in Chenonceaux, the bus stops across the street from the TI and at the château; tel. 02 47 05 30 49, www.tourainefilvert .com—click "Horaires," "Toutes les Lignes du Réseau," then "line C"); **Tours** (8/day Mon-Sat, none on Sun, buses are cheaper than trains—about €2.50).

By Shuttle Van to Chenonceaux, Chambord, and Cheverny: Quart de Tours runs two round-trips per day (summers only) between Amboise and Chenonceaux (€15 round-trip, €10 one-way, includes €2.50 discount for château, 15-minute trip), and an afternoon excursion trip from Amboise to Chambord and Cheverny (€34, allow four hours). Book ahead, as seats are limited (tel. 06 30 65 52 01, www.quartdetours.com). Check with the Amboise TI for details and pickup locations.

By Taxi: Most châteaux are too expensive by cab, but a taxi from Amboise to Chenonceaux costs about €26 (€36 on Sundays and after 19:00, tel. 02 47 57 13 53 or 02 47 57 30 39). The meter doesn't start until you do.

By Train

Within the Loire

From Amboise by Train to: **Chenonceaux** (trains are a more frequent, if slower, option than the bus; 8/day, most about 1 hour, transfer at St. Pierre-des-Corps—check connections to avoid long waits), **Blois** (14/day, 20 minutes, bus or taxi excursions from there to Chambord and Cheverny—see "Blois Connections," page 46), **Chaumont** (about 14/day, 35 minutes, take 10-minute train to Onzain on the Amboise-Blois route 25-minute walk—you can see château from station), **Tours** (12/day, 25 minutes, allows connections to châteaux west of Tours), **Chinon** (6/day, 2.25 hours, transfer in Tours and possibly in St. Pierre-des-Corps), **Azay-le-Rideau** (6/day, 2 hours, transfer in Tours and possibly in St. Pierre-des-Corps).

Beyond the Loire

Twelve 15-minute trains link Amboise daily to the regional train hub of St. Pierre-des-Corps (in suburban Tours). There you'll find reasonable connections to distant points (including the TGV to Paris' Gare Montparnasse). Transferring in Paris can be the fastest way to reach many French destinations, even in the south.

From Amboise by Train to: **Paris** (12/day, 1.5 hours to Paris' Gare Montparnasse with change to TGV at St. Pierre-des-Corps, requires TGV reservation; 6/day, 2 hours direct to Paris' Gare d'Austerlitz, no reservation required; more to Gare d'Austerlitz or Paris RER stations with same travel time and transfers in Blois or Les Aubrais-Orléans), **Sarlat** (4/day, 6 hours, several routes possible, best is to change at St. Pierre-des-Corps, then TGV to Libourne or Bordeaux-St. Jean, then train through Bordeaux vineyards to Sarlat; it's a bit slower on the route via Les Aubrais-Orléans to Souillac then scenic SNCF bus to Sarlat), **Limoges** (near Oradour-sur-Glane, 9/day, 4.5 hours, change at St. Pierre-des-Corps and Vierzon or at Les Aubrais-Orléans and Vierzon, then tricky bus connection from Limoges to Oradour-sur-Glane), **Pontorson-Mont St. Michel** (2-3/day, 5.5-7.5 hours by transfers at Caen and Tours or Rennes, Le Mans, and Tours), **Bayeux** (12/day, 4 hours by handy train via St. Pierre-des-Corps and Caen, otherwise 6 hours via St. Pierre-des-Corps and Paris' Gare Montparnasse), **Beaune** (2/day, 5 hours, transfer in Dijon; plus 12/day, 6 hours, with changes in Paris and in Dijon—arrive at Paris' Gare d'Austerlitz or Gare Montparnasse, then Métro to Gare de Lyon).

Châteaux near Amboise

1 Château de Pray
2 Château des Ormeaux &
  Château de Nazelles Chambres
3 Château des Arpentis
4 L'Auberge de Launay

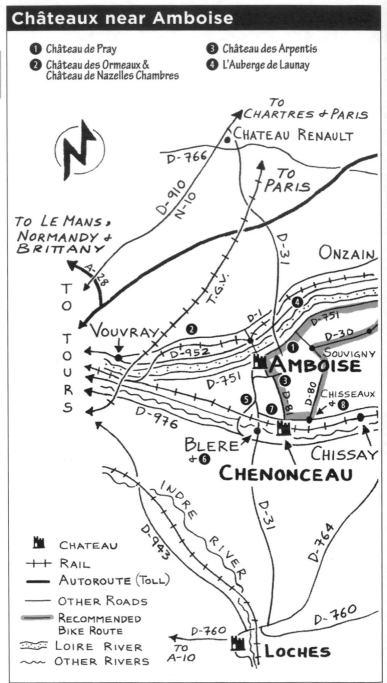

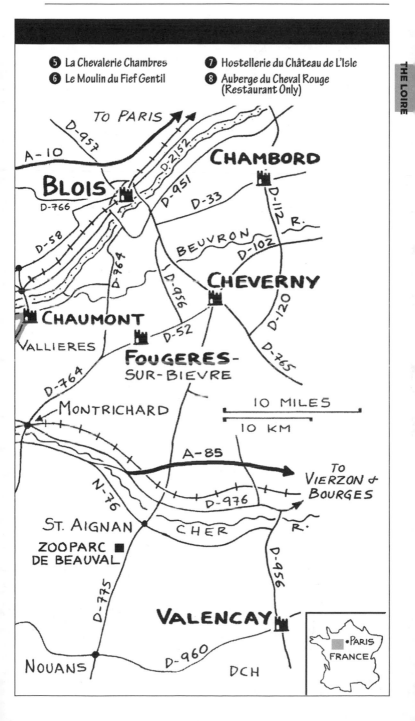

THE LOIRE

⑤ La Chevalerie Chambres
⑥ Le Moulin du Fief Gentil

⑦ Hostellerie du Château de L'Isle
⑧ Auberge du Cheval Rouge (Restaurant Only)

Chenonceaux

This one-road, sleepy village—with a knockout château—makes a good home base for drivers and a workable base for train travelers who don't mind connections. The château itself, understandably the most popular in the region, is wonderfully organized for visitors. The gardens are open on summer evenings with mood lighting and music, making the perfect after-dinner activity for those sleeping here. Note that Chenonceaux is the name of the town, and Chenonceau (no "x") is the name of the château, but they're pronounced the same: shuh-nohn-soh.

Orientation to Chenonceaux

The small **TI** is on the main road from Amboise as you enter the village. It has Wi-Fi and Internet access (July-Aug daily 9:00-19:00; Sept-June Mon-Sat 10:00-12:30 & 14:00-18:30, closed Sun; tel. 02 47 23 94 45).

The **bus** stops at the TI (the Amboise-bound stop is unsigned and across the street from the TI) and at the château (1-2 buses/day to Amboise, Mon-Sat only, none on Sun, 15 minutes).

La Maison des Pages has some bakery items, cold drinks to go, and just enough groceries for a modest picnic (on the main drag between Hostel du Roy and Hôtel la Roseraie).

You can rent **bikes** at the recommended Relais Chenonceaux hotel (May-Sept daily 9:00-19:00; see "Sleeping in Chenonceaux," later).

Sights in Chenonceaux

▲▲▲Château de Chenonceau

Chenonceau is the toast of the Loire. This 16th-century Renaissance palace arches gracefully over the Cher River and is impeccably maintained, with fresh flower arrangements in the summer and roaring log fires in the winter. Chenonceau is one of the most-visited châteaux in France—so carefully follow my crowd-beating tips, next page. Plan on a 15-minute walk from the parking lot to the château. Warning: don't leave any valuables visible in your car.

Cost and Hours: Château-€10.50, wax museum-€2, daily mid-March-mid-Sept 9:00-19:00, July-Aug until 20:00, closes earlier off-season, tel. 02 47 23 90 07, www.chenonceau.com.

Chenonceau at Night *(Promenade Nocturne):* On summer nights, floodlighting and period music create a romantic after-dinner cap to your Loire day. Just stroll over whenever and for as long as you like (€5, daily July-Aug 21:30-23:30, Fri-Sun in June).

Crowd-Beating Tips: Chenonceau's crowds are worth planning around. This place gets slammed in high season, when it's best to come early (by 9:00) or after 17:00. Avoid slow ticket lines by purchasing your ticket in advance (at area TIs) or from the ticket machines at the main entry (just follow the prompts, US credit cards work).

Tours: The interior is fascinating—but only if you take full advantage of the free, excellent 20-page **booklet** (included with entry), or rent the wonderful **iPod video/audioguide tour** (€4; two different versions available—45 or 60 minutes, each with the same stops; request the unhurried 60-minute version to enjoy full coverage). There's also an audioguide for kids. Pay for the audioguide when buying your ticket (before entering the château grounds), then pick up the iPod just inside the château's door. Or, before you visit, download the tour from www.chenonceau.com to your own iPod or other portable device for €3.

Services: WCs are available by the ticket office and behind the wax museum. There's a free bag check at the turnstile.

Wax Museum, Play Area, and Traditional Farm: The wax museum (La Galerie des Dames-Musée de Cires, located in the château stables), while tacky and designed for children, puts a waxy face on the juicy history of the château (adds €2 to ticket price, tickets only available at the château ticket office). Reading the English displays requires a series of deep knee-bends. A kids' play area *(Kindergarten)* lies just past the wax museum, and a few steps beyond that you can stroll around a traditional farm and imagine the production needed to sustain the château (free, always open).

Cuisine Art: A reasonable cafeteria is next door to the wax museum. Fancy meals are served in the orangerie behind the stables. There's a cheap *crêperie*/sandwich shop at the entrance gate. While picnics are not allowed on the grounds, there are picnic tables in a park near the parking lot.

Boat Trips: In summer, the château has rental **rowboats**—an idyllic way to savor graceful château views (€6/30 minutes, July-Aug daily 10:00-19:00, 4 people/boat).

Background: Although earlier châteaux were built for defensive purposes, Chenonceau was the first great pleasure palace. Nicknamed "the château of the ladies," it housed many famous women over the centuries. The original builder's wife oversaw the construction of the main part of the château. In 1547, King Henry II gave the château to his mistress, Diane de Poitiers, who added an arched bridge across the river to access the hunting grounds. She enjoyed her lovely retreat until Henry II died (pierced in a jousting tournament in Paris) and his vengeful wife, Catherine de Médicis, unceremoniously kicked her out (and into the château of Chaumont). Catherine added the three-story structure on Diane's bridge. She died before completing her vision of a matching château on the far side of the river, but not before turning Chenonceau into *the* place to see and be seen by local aristocracy. (Whenever you see a split coat of arms, it belongs to a woman—half her husband's and half her father's.)

○ **Self-Guided Tour:** Strut like an aristocrat down the tree-canopied path to the château. (There's a fun plant maze partway up on the left.) You'll cross three moats and two bridges, and pass an old round tower, which predates the main building. Notice the tower's fine limestone veneer, added so the top would better fit the new château.

The main château's original **oak door** greets you with the coats of arms of the first owners. The knocker is high enough to be used by visitors on horseback. The smaller door within the large one could be for two purposes: to slip in after curfew, or to enter during winter without letting out all the heat.

Once inside, you'll tour the château in a clockwise direction (turn left upon entering). Take time to appreciate the beautiful brick floor tiles and lavishly decorated ceilings. As you continue, follow your pamphlet or audioguide, and pay attention to these details:

In the **guard room,** the best-surviving original floor tiles are near the walls—imagine the entire room covered with these tiles. And though the tapestries kept the room cozy, they also functioned to tell news or recent history (to the king's liking, of course). You'll see many more tapestries in this château.

The superbly detailed **chapel** survived the vandalism of the Revolution because the fast-thinking lady of the palace filled it with firewood. Angry masses were supplied with mallets and instructions to smash everything royal or religious. While this room was both, all they saw was stacked wood. The hatch door provided a quick path to the kitchen and an escape boat downstairs. The windows, blown out during World War II, are replacements from the 1950s.

The centerpiece of the **bedroom of Diane de Poitiers** is a severe portrait of her rival, Catherine de Médicis, at 40 years old. After the queen booted out the mistress, she placed her own portrait over the fireplace, but she never used this bedroom. The 16th-century tapestries are among the finest in France. Each one took an average of 60 worker-years to make. Study the complex compositions of the *Triumph of Charity* and the violent *Triumph of Force*.

At 200 feet long, the three-story **Grand Gallery** spans the river. (The upper stories house double-decker ballrooms and art exhibits.) Notice how differently the slate and limestone of the checkered floor wear after 500 years. Imagine grand banquets here. Catherine, a contemporary of Queen Elizabeth I of England, wanted to rule with style. She threw wild parties and employed her ladies to circulate and soak up all the political gossip possible from the well-lubricated Kennedys and Rockefellers of her realm. Parties included grand fireworks displays and mock naval battles on the river. The niches once held statues—Louis XIV took a liking to them, and consequently, they now decorate the palace at Versailles.

In summer and during holidays, you can take a quick walk outside for more good palace **views:** Cross the bridge, pick up a re-entry ticket, then stroll the other bank of the Cher (across the river from the château). The river you crossed marked the border between free and Nazi France in World War II. Back then, Chenonceau witnessed many prisoner swaps. During World War I, the Grand Gallery also served as a military hospital, where more than 2,200 soldiers were cared for—picture hundreds of beds lining the gallery.

Double back through the gallery to find the sensational state-of-the-art (in the 16th century) **kitchen** below. It was built near water (to fight the inevitable kitchen fires) and in the basement; because heat rises, the placement helped heat the palace. Cross the small bridge (watch your head) to find the stove and landing bay for goods to be ferried in and out.

The staircase leading **upstairs** wowed royal guests. It was the first non-spiral staircase they'd seen...quite a treat in the 16th century. The balcony provides lovely views of the gardens—which originally supplied vegetables and herbs. (Diane built the one to the right, Catherine the one to your left.) The estate is still full of wild boar and deer—the primary dishes of past centuries. You'll see more lavish bedrooms on this floor. Find the small side rooms that show fascinating old architectural sketches of the château. The walls, 20 feet thick, were honeycombed with the flues of 224 fireplaces and passages for servants to do their pleasure-providing work unseen. There was no need for plumbing. Servants fetched, carried, and dumped everything pipes do today. The long room stretching over the river usually contains a temporary modern-art exhibit.

Sleeping in Chenonceaux

(€1 = about $1.40, country code: 33)
Hotels are a good value in Chenonceaux, and there's one in each category, from one to four stars. You'll find them *tous ensemble* on

rue du Dr. Bretonneau.

$$$ Auberge du Bon Laboureur**** makes an impression with its ivied facade and, inside, with its leathery lounges, bars, terraces, and four-star rooms at three-star prices (Db-€125-175, suites-€210-190, pool, air-con, 6 rue du Dr. Bretonneau, tel. 02 47 23 90 02, www.bonlaboureur.com, laboureur@wanadoo.fr).

$$ Hôtel la Roseraie*** has a flowery terrace and 17 warmly decorated country rooms. Sabine, Thierry, and Jerome run a good show (standard Db-€72-90, big Db-€99-129, Tb-€90-129, a few grand family rooms-€140-200, buffet breakfast-€10.50, queen- or king-size beds, air-con, free Wi-Fi, free parking, heated pool, closed Jan-Feb, 7 rue du Dr. Bretonneau, tel. 02 47 23 90 09, fax 02 47 23 91 59, www.hotel-chenonceau.com, contact@hotel-chenonceau.com). The traditional dining room and delightful terrace are ideal for a  nice dinner, available for guests and non-guests alike who reserve ahead (closed Mon and mid-Nov-mid-March).

$$ Relais Chenonceaux**, above a restaurant, greets guests with a nice patio and unimaginative, wood-paneled rooms at fair rates. The coziest—and, in summer, hottest—rooms are on the top floor, but watch your head (Db-€70, Tb-€84, Qb-€100, Wi-Fi, tel. 02 47 23 98 11, fax 02 47 23 84 07, 10 rue du Dr. Bretonneau, www.chenonceaux.com, info@chenonceaux.com).

$ Hostel du Roy* offers 32 basic budget rooms, some in a quiet garden courtyard, and a mediocre but inexpensive restaurant (Db-€46-60, Tb-€65, one-room Qb-€80, two-room Qb-€98, room for up to five-€115, Wi-Fi, 9 rue du Dr. Bretonneau, tel. 02 47 23 90 17, fax 02 47 23 89 81, www.hostelduroy.com, hostelduroy@wanadoo.fr).

Eating in and near Chenonceaux

Reserve ahead to dine in style at the country-elegant **Auberge du Bon Laboureur** (*menus* at €48, €60, and €85; tel. 02 47 23 90 02, www.bonlaboureur.com). **Hôtel la Roseraie** serves good *menus* in a stylish dining room or on a garden terrace (*menus* from €19, €5 more buys a cheese course, Tue-Sun 19:00-21:00, closed Mon and mid-Nov-mid-March). **Relais Chenonceaux** dishes up crêpes, salads, and *plats* at decent prices in a pleasant interior or on its terrace (daily). All of these are listed earlier, under "Sleeping in Chenonceaux."

For a French treat, book ahead and drive about a mile to Chisseaux and dine at the wonderfully traditional **Auberge du Cheval Rouge.** You'll enjoy some of the region's best cuisine at affordable prices, either inside or on a flower-filled patio (*menus* from €33, closed Tue-Wed, 30 rue Nationale, Chisseaux, tel. 02 47 23 86 67).

Chenonceaux Connections

From Chenonceaux by Train to: Tours (8/day, 30 minutes), with connections to **Chinon, Azay-le-Rideau,** and **Langeais; Amboise** (8/day, 1 hour, transfer at St. Pierre-des-Corps).

By Bus to: Amboise (1-2/day, Mon-Sat only, none on Sun, 20 minutes, one-way-€1.10, departs Chenonceaux at about 12:15, and in summer also at about 17:20, catch bus at the château or across the street from the TI, tel. 02 47 05 30 49, www.tourainefilvert .com).

By Shuttle Van: Quart de Tours runs two round-trips per day (summers only) between Chenonceaux and Amboise (see "Amboise Connections" on page 32).

By Taxi to: Amboise (€26, €36 on Sun and after 19:00).

Blois

Bustling Blois (pronounced "blwah") feels like a megalopolis after all those rural villages. Blois owns a rich history, dolled-up

pedestrian areas, a handsome château, and convenient access to Chambord and Cheverny by excursion bus, taxi, or car (see "Getting Around the Loire Valley" on page 5 and "Blois Connections," later). Good train service to Paris and Amboise enables easy stopovers in Blois (luggage lockers at château).

If Blois feels more important than other Loire towns, that's because it was. From this powerful city, the medieval counts of Blois governed their vast lands and vied with the king of France for dominance. The center of France moved from Amboise to Blois in 1498, when Louis XII inherited the throne (after Charles VIII had his unfortunate head-banging incident in Amboise). The château you see today is living proof of this town's 15 minutes of fame. But Blois is worth a visit for more than its château. Tour the flying-buttressed St. Nicholas Church, find the medieval warren of lanes below St. Louis Cathedral, and enjoy a café on place Louis XII.

Orientation to Blois

Unlike most other Loire châteaux, Blois' Château Royal sits right in the city center, with no forest, pond, moat, or river to call its own. It's an easy walk from the train station, near ample underground parking, and just above the TI. Below the château, place Louis XII marks the hub of traffic-free Blois, with cafés and shops lining its perimeter. Rue du Commerce, leading up from the river, is Blois' primary shopping street. Atmospheric cafés and restaurants hide in the medieval tangle of lanes below St. Louis Cathedral and around St. Nicholas Church. Blois was heavily bombed in World War II, leaving much of the old town in ruins, but the château survived. Today, the city largely ignores its river.

Arrival in Blois

Train travelers can walk 10 minutes straight out of the station down avenue Jean Laigret to the TI and château (follow small brown *Château* signs), or take a two-minute taxi from in front of the station. Although there's no bag check at the station, there are large, free **lockers** at the château—so you can drop off your luggage, visit the château and the town, and even take the excursion bus or a taxi tour to Chambord and Cheverny (provided you're back in Blois to reclaim your bag before the château closes).

Drivers follow *Centre-Ville* and *Château* signs (metered parking along avenue Jean Laigret or inside at Parking du Château—first 30 minutes free, then €2/2.5 hours).

Tourist Information

The cramped TI is across from the château entrance (daily April-Nov 9:00-18:00, Dec-March 10:00-17:00, 23 place du Château, tel. 02 54 90 41 41, www.bloispaysdechambord.com). Save time as you explore the center of Blois by using the TI's handy walking-tour brochure (brown and purple routes are best). The TI also has information on bike rentals.

Private Guide: Fabrice Maret lives in Blois and is a great teacher. He gives top-notch walking tours of his city or can join your car for a tour of area châteaux (€260/day plus transportation from Blois, tel. 02 54 70 19 59, www.chateauxloire.com, info @chateauxloire.com).

Sights in Blois

▲▲Château Royal de Blois

Unlike most other Loire châteaux, the Château Royal in Blois sits right in the city center. Even though parts of the building date from the Middle Ages, there are no defensive towers, drawbridges, or other fortifications. Gardens once extended behind the château and up the hill to the forest that ran right to the castle's back door. A walk around the building's perimeter (to the right as you face it) reveals more of its beautiful Renaissance facade.

Size up the château from the big square before entering. Kings Louis XII and François I built most of the château you see today, each calling it home during their reigns. That's Louis looking good on his horse in the niche. Catherine de Médicis (onetime owner of Chenonceau) spent her last night here, where she had been exiled by her son, Henry III.

Cost and Hours: €9.50, kids under 18-€6, €2 less off-season; €15 combo-tickets with House of Magic (described later, under "Other Sights") or sound-and-light show (see next), €20 covers all three; daily July-Aug 9:00-19:00, April-June and Sept 9:00-18:30, Oct 9:00-17:30, Nov-March 9:00-12:30 & 14:00-17:30, free lockers available with entry (same hours), tel. 02 54 90 33 33, www.chateau deblois.fr.

Sound-and-Light Show: This simple "show" takes place in the center courtyard and features projections on the château walls. An English version of the show runs on Wednesday, though the French version is worthwhile any day if you're sleeping in Blois (€7.50, €15 combo-ticket also covers daytime château entry, €20 gets you both plus the House of Magic; daily April-Sept at about 22:00).

Touring the Château: At the ticket office, pick up the helpful English brochure, then read the well-presented English displays in each room.

Begin in the **courtyard,** where four different wings—ranging from Gothic to Neoclassical—underscore this château's importance over many centuries. Stand with your back to the entry to get oriented. The medieval parts of the château are the brick-patterned sections (to your left and behind you), both built by Louis XII. François I added the elaborate Renaissance wing (to your right; early 16th century), centered on the protruding spiral staircase and festooned with his emblematic salamanders. Gaston d'Orléans inherited the place in the 1600s and wanted to do away with the mismatched styles. He demolished a large church that stood here (the chapel to your left is all that remains) and replaced it with the clean-lined, Neoclassical structure you see today.

Visit the interior counterclockwise, and focus on the Renaissance wing. Begin in the far-right corner (where you entered the courtyard) and walk under the stone porcupine relief, Louis' symbol, and up the steps into the dazzling **Hall of the Estates-General.** This is the oldest surviving part of the château (predating Louis and François), where the Estates-General met twice to help determine who would inherit the throne from Henry III, who had no male heir. (Keep reading to see how Henry resolved the problem.)

Continue into the small **lapidary museum,** with an impressive display of statues and architectural fragments from the original château; here's your chance to look nasty salamanders and gargoyles in the eye.

Next, climb upstairs to the **royal apartments of François I,** and enjoy a series of richly tiled, ornately decorated rooms with a few original furnishings. You'll see busts and portraits of some of the château's most famous residents, and near the end, learn about the dastardly 1588 murder of the duke of Guise, which took place in these apartments. In the late 1500s, the devastating Wars of Religion pitted Protestant against Catholic, and took a huge toll on this politically and religiously divided city—including the powerful Guise brothers. King Henry III (Catherine de Médicis' son) had the devoutly Catholic brothers assassinated to keep the duke off the throne.

Skip the Neoclassical wing (no English and little of interest), and end your visit with a walk through the small **fine-arts museum.** Located just over the château's entry, this 16th-century who's-who portrait gallery lets you put a face to the characters that made this château's history.

Other Sights

House of Magic (Maison de la Magie)—The home of Jean-Eugène Robert-Houdin, the illusionist whose name was adopted by Harry Houdini, offers an interesting but overpriced history of illusion and magic. Kids enjoy the gift shop. Several daily 30-minute shows have no words, so they work in any language.

Cost and Hours: Adults-€8, kids under 18-€5, €15 combo-ticket with château, €20 combo-ticket includes château and sound-and-light show; daily 9:00-12:30 & 14:00-18:30, "séance" schedule posted at entry—usually at 11:15, 15:15, and 17:15, but hours may change in summer; at the opposite end of the square from the château, tel. 02 54 90 33 33, www.maisondelamagie.fr.

Wine Cooperative—Sample wines from a variety of local vintners on the château square, next to Le Marignan café (free, 8:30-12:30 & 14:00-17:30).

Historic Center—Take time to discover Blois' pedestrian-friendly center. Although much of the old town was destroyed by WWII bombs, the area has been tastefully rebuilt. Below the castle, you'll enter a network of lively walking streets with characteristic squares, cafés and restaurants, and a few noteworthy monuments. Use the TI's self-guided tours or poke about on your own. **St. Nicholas Church,** with its flying buttresses, dates from the late 1100s and is worth a peek inside for its blend of Gothic and Romanesque styles.

The maze of medieval lanes below Blois' other hill, crowned by **St. Louis Cathedral,** are also worth a wander. **Rue du Commerce** strings smart shops along its car-free path as it climbs from the river and turns into rue de la Porte Chartraine. There's little to do along the river except to cross pont Jacques Gabriel for views back to the city.

Biking from Blois—Blois is well-positioned as a starting point for biking forays into the countryside. Cycling from Blois to Chambord is a level, 70-minute, one-way ride along a well-marked route that gets more scenic the closer you get to Chambord. You can loop back to Blois without repeating the same route, and also connect to a good network of other bike paths (the TI's free *Le Pays des Châteaux á Vélo* map shows the bike routes in this area). Adding Cheverny makes a full-day, 30-mile round-trip. The TI has info on bike-rental shops in Blois.

Sleeping in Blois

(€1 = about $1.40, country code: 33)
Blois has a scarcity of worthwhile hotels. There's a **launderette** at 6 rue St. Lubin.

 $$$ Hôtel Mercure Blois*** is modern and reliable, with a riverfront location 15 minutes from the château (Db-€120-160, air-con, 28 quai Saint Jean, tel. 02 54 56 66 66, www.mercure.com).

 $$ Best Western Blois Château*** is a better value, with stylish decor and all the comforts (Db-€85-110, Wi-Fi, loaner iPads, across from the train station and behind the château at 8 avenue du Dr. Jean Laigret, tel. 02 54 56 85 10, www.bw-bloischateau.fr, bwbloischateau@orange.fr).

 $ Hôtel Anne de Bretagne** offers budget value with 30 comfortable rooms at good prices, a central location near the château and train station, and a welcoming terrace (Sb-€46, Db-€56, Tb-€60-74, Qb-€78-84, Wi-Fi, 150 yards uphill from Parking du Château, 5-minute walk below the train station at 31 avenue Jean Laigret, tel. 02 54 78 05 38, fax 02 54 74 37 79, www.hotelannedebretagne.com, contact@hotelannedebretagne.com).

Eating in Blois

If you're stopping in Blois around lunchtime, plan on eating at **Le Marignan,** located on a breezy square in front of the château (daily, good salads and crêpes, €13-15 *menus,* fast service, 5 place du Château, tel. 02 54 74 73 15). At the top of the hour, you can watch the stately mansion opposite the château become "the dragon house," as monsters crane their long necks out its many windows.

 Between the Château and the River: The traffic-free streets

THE LOIRE

between the château and the river are home to many cafés with standard, easy meals. **Le Duc de Guise,** dishing up wood-fired pizza and basic café fare, has a favored location on place Louis XII with great outdoor seating (closed Mon, tel. 02 54 78 22 39). **La Banquette Rouge,** near St. Nicholas Church, delivers good regional cuisine with ambience to diners in long red booths—as the name suggests (€26 and €32 *menus,* closed Sun-Mon, 16 rue des Trois Marchands, tel. 02 54 78 74 92). **Le Castelet,** also near St. Nicholas, is cozy, simple, cheap, and fun, with good vegetarian choices (*menus* from €19, closed Sun and Wed, 40 rue St. Lubin, tel. 02 54 74 66 09).

Between the Cathedral and the River: Blois' most atmospheric square for an outdoor meal is place de Grenier à Sel, between the river and St. Louis Cathedral, where you'll find a few simple options; **Le Murano** does a Franco-Italian mix (closed Tue and Sat, 11 rue Vauvert, tel. 02 54 78 44 97). Nearby rue Foulerie is ground zero for hip Blois.

Blois Connections

From Blois by Train to: Amboise (14/day, 20 minutes), **Chinon** (6/day, 2-2.5 hours, transfer in Tours and possibly in St. Pierre-des-Corps), **Azay-le-Rideau** (6/day, 1.75-2.5 hours, transfer in Tours and possibly in St. Pierre-des-Corps), **Paris** (14/day, 1.5 hours).

By Bus to Chambord and Cheverny: From April through early Sept, **Transports du Loir-et-Cher** (TLC) excursion buses to Chambord, Cheverny, and (less important) Beauregard leave from the Blois train station—look for them immediately to the left as you leave the station (TLC bus marked *Navette-Châteaux*). Morning departures from Blois station at 9:10 and 11:10 go to Chambord; from Chambord, departures link Cheverny and Beauregard with various return trips to Blois, allowing you from two to seven hours at a château. Verify these times at a TI or online (€6 bus fare, good discounts offered on château entries; buy tickets and get schedule from TI or bus driver, www.tlcinfo.net).

By Taxi: Blois taxis wait 30 steps in front of the station and offer excursion fares to **Chambord, Chaumont,** or **Cheverny** (€29 one-way from Blois to one location, €92 round-trip to Chambord and Cheverny, €45 more to add Chaumont, 8-person minivans available, tel. 02 54 78 07 65). These rates are per cab, making the per-person price downright reasonable for groups of three or four.

Château de Chambord

With its huge scale and prickly silhouette, Château de Chambord, worth ▲▲, is the granddaddy of the Loire châteaux. It's surrounded

by Europe's largest enclosed forest park, a game preserve defined by a 20-mile-long wall and teeming with wild deer and boar. Chambord (shahn-bor) began as a simple hunting lodge for bored Blois counts and became a monument to the royal sport and duty of hunting. (Apparently, hunting was considered important to keep the animal population under control and the vital forests healthy.)

The château, six times the size of your average Loire castle, has 440 rooms and a fireplace for every day of the year. It consists of a keep in the shape of a Greek cross, with four towers and two wings surrounded by stables. Its four floors are each separated by 46 stairs, giving it very high ceilings. The ground floor has reception rooms, the first floor up houses the royal apartments, the second floor up houses a WWII exhibit and temporary art exhibits, and the rooftop offers a hunt-viewing terrace. Special exhibits describing Chambord at key moments in its history help animate the place. Because hunters could see best after autumn leaves fell, Chambord was a winter palace (which helps explain the 365 fireplaces). Only 80 of Chambord's rooms are open to the public—and that's plenty.

Cost and Hours: €9.50, daily April-Sept 9:00-18:15, Oct-March 9:00-17:15, last entry 30 minutes before closing, parking-€3, tel. 02 54 50 40 00, www.chambord.org. There are two ticket offices: one in the village in front of the château, and another (less crowded) inside the actual château.

Getting There: The Blois excursion bus is best (€6, two daily departures from Blois station April-early Sept, taxis from Blois are reasonable as well; see "Blois Connections," earlier, for bus and taxi details).

Information and Tours: This château requires helpful information to make it come alive. Most rooms have adequate English explanations. You can rent an audioguide for a thorough history of the château and its rooms (€5, two can share one audioguide with volume turned to max). Or, before you visit, download the tour from www.podibus.com to your own iPod or other portable device for free.

Services: The bookshop in the château has a good selection of children's books. Among the collection of shops near the château, you'll find a TI (April-Oct daily 9:30-13:00 & 14:00-18:00, closed Nov-March, tel. 02 54 33 39 16), an ATM, WCs, local souvenirs, a wine-tasting room, and cafés. There's only one WC at the château itself (in a courtyard corner).

Biking Around the Park: You can rent bikes (€6/hour, €8/2 hours) to explore the park—a network of leafy lanes crisscrossing the vast expanse contained within its 20-mile-long wall.

Medieval Pageantry on Horseback Show: The 45-minute, family-friendly show (in the stables across the field from the château entry) is high-powered and full of clanging swords and pikes—performed on horseback and in medieval armor. Afterwards, the knights and horses come out to mingle and chat with children (€15; July-Aug daily at 11:45 and 16:30, May-June and Sept-early Oct Tue-Sun at 11:45, Sat-Sun also at 16:30, closed Mon; tel. 02 54 20 31 01, www.ecuries-chambord.com).

Views: For the best views, cross the small river in front of the château and turn right. The recommended Hôtel du Grand St. Michel has a broad view terrace, ideal for post-château refreshment.

Background: Starting in 1518, François I created this "weekend retreat," employing 1,800 workmen for 15 years. (You'll see his signature salamander symbol everywhere.) François I was an absolute monarch—with an emphasis on absolute. In 32 years of rule (1515-1547), he never once called the Estates-General to session (a rudimentary parliament in *ancien régime* France). This grand hunting palace was another way to show off his power. Countless guests, like Charles V—the Holy Roman Emperor and most powerful man of the age—were invited to this pleasure palace of French kings...and were totally wowed.

The grand architectural plan of the château—modeled after an Italian church—feels designed as a place to worship royalty. Each floor of the main structure is essentially the same: four equal arms of a Greek cross branch off of a monumental staircase, which leads up to a cupola. From a practical point of view, the design pushed the usable areas to the four corners. This castle, built while the pope was erecting a new St. Peter's Basilica, is like a secular rival to the Vatican.

Construction started the year Leonardo died, 1519. The architect is unknown, but an eerie Leonardo-esque spirit resides here. The symmetry, balance, and classical proportions combine to reflect a harmonious Renaissance vision that could have been inspired by Leonardo's notebooks.

Typical of royal châteaux, this palace of François I was rarely used. Because any effective king had to be on the road to exercise his power, royal palaces sat empty most of the time. In the 1600s, Louis XIV renovated Chambord, but he visited it only six times (for about two weeks each visit).

❍ Self-Guided Tour: This tour covers the highlights, floor by floor.

Ground Floor: This stark level shows off the general plan—four wings, small doors to help heated rooms stay warm, and a massive staircase. In a room just inside the front door, on the left, you can watch a worthwhile 18-minute video.

The attention-grabbing **double-helix staircase** dominates the open vestibules and invites visitors to climb up. Its two spirals are interwoven, so people can climb up and down and never meet. From the staircase, enjoy fine views of the vestibule action, or just marvel at the playful Renaissance capitals carved into its light tuff stone.

First Floor: Here you'll find the most interesting rooms. Starting opposite a big ceramic stove, tour this floor basically clockwise. You'll enter the lavish apartments in the **king's wing** and pass through the grand bedrooms of Louis XIV, his wife Maria Theresa, and, at the far end, François I (follow *Logis de François 1er* signs). Notice how the furniture in François' bedroom was designed to be easily disassembled and moved with him.

A highlight of the first floor is the fascinating seven-room **Museum of the Count of Chambord** (Musée du Comte de Chambord). The last of the French Bourbons, the count of Chambord was next in line to be king when France decided it didn't need one. He was raring to rule—you'll see his coronation outfits and even souvenirs from the coronation that never happened. Check out his boyhood collection of little guns, including a working mini-cannon. The man who believed he should have become King Henry V lived in exile from the age of 10. Although he opened the palace to the public, he actually visited this château only once, in 1871.

The **chapel** tucked off in a side wing is interesting only for how unimpressive it is. It's dwarfed by the mass of this imposing château, clearly designed to trumpet the glories not of God, but of the king of France.

Second Floor: Beneath beautiful coffered ceilings (notice the "F" for François) is a series of ballrooms that once hosted post-hunt parties. From here, you'll climb up to the rooftop, but first lean to the center of the staircase and look down its spiral.

Rooftop: A pincushion of spires and chimneys decorates the rooftop viewing terrace. From a distance, the roof—with its frilly forest of stone towers—gives the massive château a deceptive lightness. From here, ladies could scan the estate grounds, enjoying the spectacle of their ego-pumping men out hunting. On hunt day, a line of beaters would fan out and work inward from the distant walls, flushing wild game to the center, where the king and his buddies waited. The showy lantern tower of the tallest spire glowed with a nighttime torch when the king was in.

Gaze up at the grandiose tip-top of the tallest tower, capped with the king's fleur-de-lis symbol. It's a royal lily—not a cross—that caps this monument to the power of the French king.

In the Courtyard: Leaving the main part of the château, turn left. In the corner (just past the summer café), a door leads to the classy **carriage rooms** and the fascinating **lapidary rooms.** Here you'll come face-to-face with original stonework from the roof, including the graceful lantern cupola, with the original palace-capping fleur-de-lis. Imagine having to hoist that load. The volcanic tuff stone used to build the spires was soft and easy to work, but not very durable—particularly when so exposed to the elements.

Sleeping near Chambord and Cheverny

(€1 = about $1.40, country code: 33)
$$ Hôtel du Grand St. Michel** lets you wake up with Chambord outside your window. It's an Old World, hunting-lodge kind of place with rooms in pretty good shape and a trophy-festooned dining room (*menus* from €20). Sleep here and you'll have a chance to roam the château grounds after the peasants have been run out (small Db-€62-72, bigger Db-€75, Db facing château-€85-115 and worth the extra euros, Tb-€95-120, extra bed-€15, tel. 02 54 20 31 31, fax 02 54 20 36 40, on place Saint Louis, www.saintmichel-chambord.com, hotelsaintmichel@wanadoo.fr).

$$ Chambres la Flânerie, on the bike route from Chambord to Cheverny, offers two family rooms in an adorable home. It's riddled with flowers, crawling with ivy, and surrounded by wheat fields and forests. The gentle Delabarres speak enough English and loan bikes to their fortunate guests (Db-€62, Tb-€80, Qb-€96, includes breakfast, 25 rue de Gallerie, tel. 02 54 79 86 28, mobile 06 75 72 28 41, www.laflanerie.com, laflanerie@laflanerie.com). Coming from Blois on D-765, it's before Cheverny in the hamlet of Les Fées. Turn right where you see wooden bus shelters flanking the road, and follow signs to *Eric Auge Menuiserie.*

Cheverny

This stately hunting palace, a ▲▲ sight, is one of the more lavishly furnished Loire châteaux. Because the immaculately preserved Cheverny (shuh-vehr-nee) was built and decorated in a relatively short 30 years, from 1604 to 1634, it offers a unique architectural harmony and unity of style. From the start, this château has been in the Hurault family, and Hurault pride shows in its flawless pres-

ervation and intimate feel. The viscount's family still lives on the third floor (not open to the public, but you'll see some family photos). Cheverny was spared by the French Revolution; the owners were popular then, as today, even among the village farmers.

The château is flanked by a pleasant village, with a small grocery, cafés offering good lunch options, and a few hotels. You can get to Cheverny by bus from Blois (see "Blois Connections" on page 46) or by minivan tour from Amboise (see "Getting Around the Loire Valley" on page 5).

Cost and Hours: €8, family deals, daily July-Aug 9:15-19:00, April-June and Sept 9:15-18:15, Oct 9:45-17:30, Nov-March 9:45-17:00, tel. 02 54 79 96 29, www.chateau-cheverny.fr.

Touring the Château: As you walk across the manicured grounds toward the gleaming château, the sound of hungry hounds will follow you. Medallions with portraits of Roman emperors, including Julius Caesar (above the others in the center), line up across the facade. As you enter the château, pick up the excellent English self-guided tour brochure, which describes the interior beautifully.

Your visit starts in the lavish **dining room,** decorated with

leather walls and a sumptuous ceiling. As you climb the stairs to the private apartments, look out the window and spot the orangerie across the grass. It was here that the *Mona Lisa* was hidden (along with other treasures from the Louvre) during World War II.

On the first floor up, you'll tour the I-could-live-here **family apartments** with silky bedrooms, kids' rooms, and an intimate dining room.

You'll pass though the **Arms Room** before landing in the **King's Bedchamber**—literally fit for a king. Study the fun ceiling art, especially the "boys will be boys" cupids. Following the tour booklet, in later rooms, find a grandfather clock with a second hand that's been ticking for 250 years, a family tree going back to 1490, and a letter of thanks from George Washington to this family for their help in booting out the English.

Nearby: Barking dogs remind visitors that the viscount still loves to hunt. The **kennel** (200 yards in front of the château, look for *Chenil* signs) is especially interesting at dinnertime, when the 70 hounds are fed (April-mid-Sept daily at 17:00, mid-Sept-March Mon and Wed-Fri at 15:00). The dogs—half English foxhound and half French Poitou—are bred to have big feet and bigger stamina. They're given food once a day, and the feeding *(la soupe des chiens)* is a fun spectacle that shows off their strict training. Before chow time, the hungry hounds fill the little kennel rooftop and watch the trainer bring in troughs stacked with delectable raw meat. He opens the gate, and the dogs gather enthusiastically around the food, yelping hysterically. Only when the trainer says to eat can they dig in. You can see the dogs at any time, but the feeding show is fun to plan for.

Also nearby, **Tintin** comic-lovers can enter a series of fun rooms designed to take them into a Tintin adventure (called Les Secrets de Moulinsart, €12 combo-ticket with castle); hunters can inspect an antler-filled **trophy room;** and gardeners can prowl the château's fine **kitchen and flower gardens** (free, behind the dog kennel).

Wine-Tastings at the Château Gate: Opposite the entry to the château sits a slick wine-tasting room, **La Maison des Vins.** It's run by an association of 32 local vintners. Their mission: to boost the Cheverny reputation for wine (which is fruity, light, dry, and aromatic compared to the heavier, oaky wines made farther downstream). Tasters have two options. In the first, any visitor can have four free tastes from featured bottles of the day, offered with helpful guidance. Or, for a fee, you can sample more freely among the 32 labels, at your own pace, by using modern automated dispensers. Even if just enjoying the free samples, wander among the spouts. Each gives the specs of that wine in English (€6.50 for small tastes of 7 wines, €6-9 bottles, daily 11:00-19:00, tel. 02 54 79 25 16, www.maisondesvinsdecheverny.fr).

Fougères-sur-Bièvre

The feudal castle of Fougères-sur-Bièvre (foo-zher sewr bee-ehv) dominates its hamlet and is worth a stop, even if you don't go inside (but I would). Located a few minutes from Cheverny on the way to Chenonceaux and Amboise, Fougères-sur-Bièvre was constructed for defense, not hunting. It was built over a small river to provide an unlimited water supply during sieges. Leveled in the Hundred Years' War, then rebuilt in the 1500s, it's completely restored. Although there are no furnishings (there weren't many in the Middle Ages in any case), it gives you a good look at how castles were built.

Follow the route with the helpful English handout (brief

English explanations are also provided in most rooms). You'll see models of castle-construction techniques, including interesting exhibits on the making of half-timbered walls (oak posts and cross-beams provided the structural skeleton, and the areas in between were filled in with a mix of clay, straw, and pebbles). Walk under medieval roof supports, gaze through loopholes, and stand over machicolations (holes for dropping rocks and scalding liquids on attackers) in the main tower. Seeing the main tower from within adds an entirely new appreciation of these structures' complexity, and the two medieval latrines demonstrate how little toilet technology has changed in 800 years. Before leaving, take a few minutes to visit the re-created medieval vegetable garden.

Cost and Hours: €5; May-mid-Sept daily 9:30-12:30 & 14:00-18:30; mid-Sept-April Wed-Mon 10:00-12:00 & 14:00-17:00, closed Tue; last entry 30 minutes before closing, tel. 02 54 20 27 18, http://fougeres-sur-bievre.monuments-nationaux.fr.

Getting There: Fougères-sur-Bièvre has no easy public-transport link from Amboise...or anywhere else. If you're *sans* rental car or bike, arrange for a custom minivan tour—or skip it.

Chaumont-sur-Loire

A castle has been located on this spot since the 11th century; the current version is a ▲▲ sight. The first priority at Chaumont

(show-mon) was defense. You'll appreciate the strategic location on the long climb up from the village below. (Drivers can avoid the uphill hike except off-season—explained later.) Gardeners will appreciate the elaborate Festival of Gardens that unfolds next to the château every year, and modern-art lovers will enjoy how works have been incorporated into the gardens, château, and stables.

Cost and Hours: Château and stables-€9.50; château open daily July-Aug 10:00-19:00, May-June and early Sept 10:00-18:00, April and late Sept 10:30-17:30, Oct-March 10:00-17:00, last entry 30 minutes before closing; stables close daily 12:00-14:00; English handout available, tel. 02 54 20 99 22, www.domaine-chaumont.fr.

Festival of Gardens: This annual exhibit, with 25 elaborate gardens arranged around a different theme each year, draws rave reviews from international gardeners (Garden Festival-€10; château, stables, and Garden Festival-€15; May-mid-Oct daily 10:00-20:00, tel. 02 54 20 99 22, www.domaine-chaumont.fr). When the festival is on, you'll find several little cafés and reasonable lunch options scattered about the festival hamlet (festival ticket not needed).

Getting There: There is no public transport to Chaumont, although the train between Blois and Amboise can drop you in Onzain, a 25-minute walk across the river to the château (8/day). Bikes, taxis (reasonable from Blois train station), and chartered minivans also work for non-drivers (see "Getting Around the Loire Valley" on page 5).

From May to mid-October, drivers can park up top, at an entrance open only during the Festival of Gardens (you don't need to buy tickets for the garden event). From the river, drive up behind the château (direction: Montrichard), take the first hard right turn (following *Stade du Tennis* signs), and drive to the lot beyond the soccer field.

Background: The Chaumont château you see today was built mostly in the 15th and 16th centuries. Catherine de Médicis forced Diane de Poitiers to swap Chenonceau for Chaumont; you'll see tidbits about both women inside. Louis XVI, Marie-Antoinette, Voltaire, and Benjamin Franklin all spent time here. Today's château offers a good look at the best defense design in 1500: on a cliff with a dry moat, big and small drawbridges with classic ramparts, loopholes for archers, and handy holes through which to dump hot oil on attackers.

⊃ Self-Guided Tour: There's no audioguide or regular English tour. Your walk through the palace—restored mostly in the 19th century—is described by the English flier you'll pick up when you enter. As the château has more rooms than period furniture, your tour will be peppered with modern-art exhibits that fill otherwise empty spaces. The rooms you'll visit first (in the east wing) show the château as it appeared in the 15th and 16th centuries. Your visit ends in the west wing, which features furnishings from the 19th-century owners.

The castle's medieval **entry** is littered with various coats of arms. As you walk in, take a close look at the two drawbridges (a new mechanism allows the main bridge to be opened with the touch of a button). Once inside, the heavy defensive feel is replaced with palatial luxury. Peek into the courtyard—during the more stable 1700s, the fourth wing, which had enclosed the courtyard, was taken down to give the terrace its river-valley view.

Entering the château rooms, signs direct you along a one-way loop path *(suite de la visite)* through the château's three wings. Catherine de Médicis, who missed her native Florence, brought a touch of Italy to all her châteaux, and her astrologer (Ruggieri) was so important that he had his own (plush) room—next to hers.

Catherine's bedroom has a case with ceramic portrait busts dating from 1770, when the lord of the house had a tradition of welcoming guests by having their portrait sketched, then giving them a ceramic bust made from this sketch when they departed. Find Ben Franklin's medallion. The exquisitely tiled **Salle de Conseil** has a grand fireplace designed to keep this conference room warm. The treasury box in the **guard room** is a fine example of 1600s-era locksmithing. The lord's wealth could be locked up here as safely as possible in those days, with a false keyhole, no handles, and even an extra-secure box inside for diamonds.

A big spiral staircase leads up through a messy attic and then down to rooms decorated in 19th-century style. The **dining room**'s fanciful limestone fireplace is exquisitely carved. Find the food (frog legs, snails, goats for cheese), the maid with the bellows, and even the sculptor with a hammer and chisel at the top (on the left). Your visit ends with a stroll through the 19th-century library, the billiards room, and the living room.

In the **courtyard,** study the entertaining spouts and decor on the walls.

The **stables** *(ecuries)* were entirely rebuilt in the 1880s. The medallion above the gate reads *pour l'avenir* (for the future), which shows off an impressive commitment to horse technology. Inside, circle clockwise—you can almost hear the clip-clop of horses walking. Notice the deluxe horse stalls, padded with bins and bowls for hay, oats, and water, complete with a strategically placed drainage gutter. The horses were named for Greek gods and great châteaux. The Horse Kitchen (Cuisine des Chevaux) produced mash twice weekly for the horses. The "finest tack room in all of France" shows off horse gear. Beyond the covered alcove where the horse and carriage were prepared for the prince, you'll see four carriages parked and ready to go. Finally, the round former kiln was redesigned to be a room for training the horses.

The estate is a **tree garden,** set off by a fine lawn. Trees were imported from throughout the Mediterranean world to be enjoyed—and to fend off any erosion on this strategic bluff.

Loches and Valençay

Loches

The overlooked town of Loches (lohsh), located about 30 minutes south of Amboise, makes a good base for drivers wanting to visit sights east and west of Tours (in effect triangulating between Amboise and Chinon), but has no easy train or bus connections. This pretty town sits on the region's loveliest river, the Indre, and holds an appealing mix of medieval monuments, stroll-worthy

THE LOIRE

streets, and fewer tourists. Its château dominates the skyline and is worth a short visit. The Wednesday and Saturday street markets are lively; the Saturday market takes over many streets in the old city.

Sleeping in Loches: For an overnight stay, try **$$ Hôtel George Sand*****, located on the river, with a well-respected restaurant, an idyllic terrace, and rustic, comfortable rooms (Db-€60-72, luxury Db-€135, Tb-€95, Wi-Fi, no elevator, 300 yards south of TI at 39 rue Quintefol, tel. 02 47 59 39 74, fax 02 47 91 55 75, www.hotel restaurant-georgesand.com, contactGS@hotelrestaurant-george sand.com). **$$$ Le Logis du Bief,** a fine, welcoming *chambre d'hôte* in the center of town with four lovely, air-conditioned rooms, has a riverfront terrace and cozy living spaces (Db-€80-95, Tb-€120, includes breakfast, 21 Rue Quintefol, tel. 02 47 91 66 02, mobile 06 83 10 46 64, www.logisloches.com).

Valençay

The Renaissance château of Valençay (vah-lahn-say) is a massive, luxuriously furnished structure with echoes of its former owner Talleyrand (Napoleon's prime minister) and lovely gardens. It has kid-friendly activities and elaborate big toys, and lots of summer events such as fencing demonstrations and candlelit visits.

Cost and Hours: €11, ask about family rates, free audioguide covers château and gardens, daily June 9:30-18:30, July-Aug 9:30-19:00, April-May and Sept 10:00-18:00, Oct 10:20-17:30, closed Nov-March, tel. 02 54 00 15 69, www.chateau-valencay.fr.

West of Tours

Chinon

This pleasing town straddles the Vienne River and hides its ancient streets under a historic royal fortress. Today's Chinon (shee-nohn) is better known for its popular red wines. But for me it makes the best home base for seeing the sights west of Tours: Azay-le-Rideau (sound-and-light show), Langeais, Villandry, Chatonnière, Rivau, Ussé, and the Abbaye Royale de Fontevraud. Each of these worthwhile sights is no more than a 20-minute drive away. Trains provide access to many châteaux but are time-consuming, so you're better off with your own car or a minivan excursion (see "Getting Around the Loire Valley," on page 5, and "Chinon Connections," later).

Orientation to Chinon

Chinon stretches out along the Vienne River, and everything of interest to travelers lies between it and the hilltop fortress. Charming place du Général de Gaulle—ideal for café-lingering—is in the center of town.

Tourist Information

The TI is in the town center, near the base of the hill and a 15-minute walk from the train station. You'll find *chambre d'hôte* listings, wine-tasting details (wine-route maps available for the serious taster), bike-rental information, and an English-language self-guided tour of the town (May-Sept daily 10:00-19:00; Oct-April Mon-Sat 10:00-12:00 & 14:00-18:00, closed Sun; in village center on place Hofheim, tel. 02 47 93 17 85, www.chinon-valde loire.com). Free public WCs are around the back of the TI.

Helpful Hints

Market Days: A market takes place all day Thursday on place Jeanne d'Arc (west end of town). There's a sweet little market on Sunday, around place du Général de Gaulle.

Groceries: Carrefour City is across from the Hôtel de Ville, on place du Général de Gaulle (Mon-Sat 7:00-20:00, Sun 9:00-13:00).

Laundry: Salon Lavoir is near the bridge at #7 quai Charles VII (daily 7:00-21:00).

Bike and Canoe Rental: Canoe-Kayak & Vélo rents bikes and canoes on the river, next to the campground (bikes-€14/day; canoes-€9.50/2 hours or €17/half-day, shuttle included; €21 to combine bike and canoe in a full day; tel. 06 23 82 96 33, www.loisirs-nature.fr).

Taxi: Call 02 47 58 46 58 or mobile 06 89 47 56 08.

Car Rental: It's best to book a car at the St. Pierre-des-Corps train station in Tours.

Best Views: You'll find terrific rooftop views from rue du Coteau St. Martin (between St. Mexme Church and the fortress—see map), and rewarding river views to Chinon by crossing the bridge in the center of town and turning right (small river-front café May-Sept).

Self-Guided Walk

Welcome to Chinon

Chinon offers a peaceful world of quiet cobbled lanes, historic buildings, and few tourists. By following this walk (or the TI's self-guided tour brochure) and reading plaques at key build-

Chinon

1. Best Western Hôtel de France & Le Café des Arts
2. Hôtel Diderot
3. Le Plantagenet Hôtel
4. Hôtel Agnès Sorel
5. Hôtel la Treille & Rest.
6. La Bonne France Rest.
7. L'Océanic Restaurant & La Saladerie-Crêperie
8. Restaurant-Musée Animé du Vin et de la Tonnellerie
9. La Cave Voltaire Wine-Tastings
10. Caves Painctes Wine-Tastings
11. Caves Plouzeau Wine-Tastings
12. Café Français
13. Panoramic Elevator
14. Launderette
15. Bike/Canoe Rental
16. Grocery Store

◀ VIEW   P PARKING

ings, you'll gain a good understanding of this city's historic importance.

Begin this quick walk in the town center on the main square, **place du Général de Gaulle.** In medieval times, as was typical of that age, the market was here, just outside the town wall. The town hall building, originally an arcaded market, was renovated only in the 19th century. Today it flies three flags: Europe, France, and Chinon (with its three castles). From here, you can see the handy elevator that connects the town with its castle.

Side-trip down to the **Vienne River.** The town wall once sat on the wide swath of land running from the square down to the river, effectively walling the city off from the water—and explaining why, even now, Chinon seems to turn its back on its river.

A statue on the embankment honors the famous Renaissance writer and satirist **François Rabelais,** who was born here in 1494. You'll see many references to him in his proud town. His best-known works, *Gargantua* and *Pantagruel,* which describe the amusing adventures of father-and-son giants, were set in Chinon.

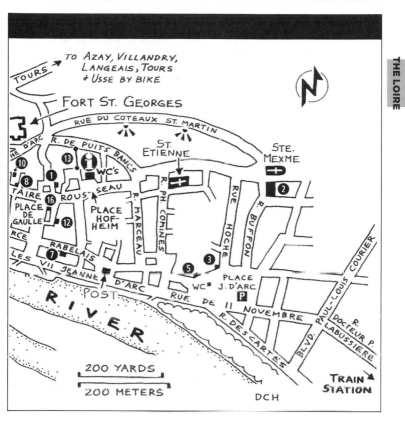

Rabelais' vivid humor and savage wit are, for many, quintessentially French—there's even a French word for it: *rabelaisien*. With his bawdy books, Rabelais critiqued society in ways others could not get away with. A monk and a doctor, he's considered the first great French novelist, and his farces were a voice against the power of Church and king.

Return to place de Gaulle and turn left down **rue Voltaire.** If the old wall still stood, you'd be entering town through the east gate. (Note the black info posts here and scattered throughout town.) Walk along a fine strip of 16th-, 17th-, and 18th-century houses. A few steps to the right on rue du Dr. Gendron is the charming little **Musée Animé du Vin;** at the next corner is **Cave Voltaire** (both described later).

Walk farther into the **old town.** In the immediate post-WWII years, there was little money or energy to care for beautiful old towns. But in the 1960s, new laws and sensitivities kicked in, and old quarters like this were fixed up and preserved. Study the vernacular architecture. La Maison Rouge (at 38-42 rue Voltaire) is a fine example of the town's medieval structures: a stone foundation and timber frame, filled in with whatever was handy. With dense populations crowding within the protective town walls, buildings swelled wider at top to avoid blocking congested streets.

Pop into the ancient **bookshop** on the corner. I asked the owner where he got old prints. He responded, "Did you ever enjoy a friend's mushrooms and ask him where he found them? Did he tell you?"

The **town museum** is across the street. Its plaque recalls that this building housed an Estates-General meeting, convened by Charles VII, in 1428. Just around the corner, find a good castle view (and a public WC).

Sights in Chinon

▲Forteresse Royale de Chinon

Chinon's castle (or fortress) is more ruined and older than the more famous and visited châteaux of the Loire. It comes without a hint of pleasure palace. While there's not much left, its rich history makes the castle a popular destination for French tourists and school groups.

Cost and Hours: €7, daily May-Aug 9:30-19:00, April and Sept 9:30-18:00, Oct-March 9:30-17:00, tel. 02 47 93 13 45, www.forteressechinon.fr.

Castle Tours: Your admission includes a free audio tour. Free English-language tours leave daily (45 minutes, generally at 11:00, 14:00, and 17:00).

Getting There: It's a bracing walk up from town, or you can take the free "panoramic" elevator from behind the TI. You'll find a free parking lot 100 yards above the castle entry.

Background: Henry II and Eleanor of Aquitaine, who ruled a vast realm from Scotland to the Spanish border, reigned from here around 1150. They had eight children (among them two future kings, including Richard the Lionhearted). And it was in this castle that Joan of Arc pleaded with Charles VII to muster the courage to rally the French and take the throne back from the nasty English. Charles had taken refuge in this well-fortified castle during the Hundred Years' War, making Chinon France's capital city during that low ebb in Gallic history.

Touring the Castle: The castle has three structures separated by moats. You'll enter via the oldest part, the 12th-century Fort Saint-Georges. Crossing a dry moat, you find yourself in the big courtyard of the Château du Milieu; at the far end is Fort Coudray.

Follow the arrows through eight stark and stony rooms, enjoying the clever teaching videos. There's a small museum devoted to the legendary Joan of Arc and her myth, developed through the centuries to inspire the French to pride and greatness. The fort comes with commanding views of town, the river, and the château-studded countryside. Chinon—both the city and the castle—developed as its political importance grew. It was the seat of French royalty in the 14th century. Most of the stones were quarried directly below the castle and hauled up through a well. The resulting caverns keep stores of local wine cool to this day.

Wine Sights and Tastings in and near Chinon

Chinon reds are among the most respected in the Loire, and there are a variety of ways to sample them.

The most convenient is at **La Cave Voltaire,** where cool, English-speaking sommelier Patrice would love to help you learn about his area's wines. He serves inexpensive appetizers and has wines from all regions of France (daily 10:00-22:00, near place du Général de Gaulle at 13 rue Voltaire, tel. 02 47 93 37 68).

Caves Painctes gives you a chance to sample Chinon wines, as well as to walk through the cool quarry from which stones for the castle and town's houses were cut. This rock (tuff) is soft and easily quarried, and when exposed to oxygen, it hardens. The *caves*, 300 feet directly below the castle, were dug as the castle was built. Its stones were hauled directly up to the building site with a treadmill-powered hoist (think Mont St. Michel, if you've visited there). Converted to wine cellars in the 15th century, the former quarry is a pilgrimage site of sorts for admirers of Rabelais, who featured it prominently in his writings. To visit, you must sign up for a tour, which takes about an hour and includes a 10-minute video and a tasting of three local wines. Designed to promote Chinon wines, it's run by a local winemakers' association (€3, four admissions/day July-Aug only at 11:00, 15:00, 16:30, and 18:00, closed Mon, off rue Voltaire on impasse des Caves Painctes, tel. 02 47 93 30 44).

Caves Plouzeau offers another opportunity to walk through long, atmospheric caves—complete with mood lighting—that extend under the château to a (literally) cool tasting room and reasonably priced wines (€6-11/bottle, April-Sept Tue-Sat 11:00-13:00 & 15:00-19:00, closed Sun-Mon and Oct-March, at the western end of town on 94 rue Haute St-Maurice, tel. 02 47 93 16 34).

Restaurant-Musée Animé du Vin et de la Tonnellerie ("Wine and Barrel Museum and Restaurant") is the life's work of a passionate wine-lover, the mustachioed Dédé la Boulange. You'll stroll through a few rooms animated by characters re-creating the production of local wines, and smile at the ingenuity of his handiwork (€4.50, €2.50 if you enjoy dinner at his recommended restaurant on the premises, daily mid-March–mid-Oct 10:00-22:00, closed off-season, 12 rue Voltaire).

Near Chinon: For an authentic winery experience in the thick of the vineyards, drive about 25 minutes from Chinon to **Domaine de la Chevalerie.** This traditional winery has been run by the same family for 14 generations. Fun-loving and English-speaking daughter Stéphanie will take you through the cavernous hillside cellars crammed with 260,000 bottles, then treat you to a tasting of their 100 percent Cabernet Franc reds from seven different plots of land (daily 10:00-12:00 & 14:00-19:00, best to call ahead, off D-35 at 7 rue du Peu Muleau, Restigné, tel. 02 47 97 46 32, www .domainedelachevalerie.fr).

Other Sights

▲**Biking from Chinon**—Many good options are available from Chinon. Most cyclists can manage the pleasant ride from Chinon to Ussé. To avoid a monumental hill, take your bike in the free elevator behind the TI up to the château level, and follow *Loire à Vélo* signs (route #4 on their map). You'll come to a quiet lane that crosses the Indre River, then follow the Loire River to Langeais and Villandry. After Villandry, the path follows the Cher River into Tours. Connecting these three châteaux towns is a full-day, 40-mile round-trip ride that only those in fit condition will enjoy. (See "Helpful Hints," earlier, for rental location and costs.)

Canoeing/Kayaking from Chinon—From May through September, you'll find plastic canoes and kayaks for rent next to the campground across the lone bridge in Chinon. The outfitters will shuttle you upriver to tiny Anché for a scenic and fun two-hour, four-mile float back to town—ending with great Chinon fortress views. They also offer a 10-mile, half-day float that starts in Chinon and ends downriver in the lovely village of Candes-St.-Martin. Or do your own biathlon by canoeing one way and biking back (see "Helpful Hints," earlier, for rental location and costs).

Nighttime in Chinon—**Café Français** has live music several nights a week. Run by Jean François (a.k.a. "Jeff"), it's a character-istic local hangout and *the* place for any late-night fun in this sleepy town (open Tue-Sat from 18:00 and Sun from 19:00 until you shut it down, closed Mon, behind town hall at 37 rue des Halles, tel. 02 47 93 32 78).

Sleeping in Chinon

(€1 = about $1.40, country code: 33)
Hotels are a good value in Chinon. If you stay overnight here, walk out to the river and cross the bridge for a floodlit view of the château walls.

$$$ Best Western Hôtel de France*** offers sufficient comfort without the personal touches of the other hotels I list. Still, I like the location—at Chinon's best square—as well as the open patios and half-timbered hallways inside the hotel (Db-€109-148, most are about €124, Tb/Qb-€148-178, includes breakfast, several rooms have balconies over the square, some have thin walls, Wi-Fi, 49 place du Général de Gaulle, tel. 02 47 93 33 91, fax 02 47 98 37 03, www.bestwestern-hoteldefrance-chinon.com, elma chinon@aol.com).

$$ Hôtel Diderot** is the place to stay in Chinon. This handsome 18th-century manor house on the eastern edge of town is the

closest hotel I list to the train station (drivers, look for signs from place Jeanne d'Arc). It's a family affair, run by spirited Laurent and his equally spirited sisters, Françoise and Martine, who will adopt you into their clan if you're not careful. The hotel surrounds a carefully planted courtyard, and has a full bar with a good selection of area wines. Rooms in the main building vary in size and decor, but all are well-maintained, with personal touches. Ground-floor rooms are a bit dark, but they have private patios. The four good family rooms have connecting rooms, each with a private bathroom. Breakfast (€9) includes a rainbow of homemade jams (Sb-€60-68, Db-€66-86, extra bed-€12, Wi-Fi, limited parking-€7/day, 4 rue de Buffon, tel. 02 47 93 18 87, fax 02 47 93 37 10, www.hoteldiderot.com, hoteldiderot@wanadoo.fr).

$$ Le Plantagenet has 30 sufficiently comfortable rooms and may have space when others don't (Db-€66-71 without air-con, Db-€81 with air-con, some rooms have balconies, 12 place Jeanne d'Arc, tel. 02 47 93 36 92, www.hotel-plantagenet.com, resa @hotel-plantagenet.com).

$ Hôtel Agnès Sorel, at the western end of town, sits on the river and is handy for drivers, but it's a 30-minute walk from the train station and has some traffic noise. Of its ten sharp rooms, three have river views, two have balconies, and five surround a small courtyard. A few are air-conditioned (Db-€50-60, bigger Db-€80, big Db suite-€100, T/Qb suite-€120, Wi-Fi in lobby, 4 quai Pasteur, tel. 02 47 93 04 37, fax 02 47 93 06 37, www.hotel -agnes-sorel.com, christine.tarre@hotel-agnes-sorel.com).

$ Hôtel la Treille has five rugged and rustic rooms for budget travelers (Db-€42, Tb-€52, 4 place Jeanne d'Arc, tel. 02 47 93 07 71, no fax, no email, no overhead).

Outside Chinon, near Ligré

$$$ Le Clos de Ligré lets you sleep in farmhouse silence, surrounded by vineyards and farmland. A 10-minute drive from Chinon, it has room to roam, a pool overlooking the vines, and a billiards room with a baby grand piano. English-speaking Martine Descamps spoils her guests with cavernous and creatively decorated rooms (Db-€110, good family rooms, includes breakfast, €35 dinner includes the works, cash only, 37500 Ligré, tel. 02 47 93 95 59, mobile 06 61 12 45 55, www.le-clos-de-ligre.com, martinedescamps@le-clos-de-ligre.com). From Chinon, cross the river and go toward Richelieu on D-760, turn right on D-115, and continue for about five kilometers (three miles). Turn left, following signs to *Ligré,* and look for signs to *Le Clos de Ligré.*

Eating in Chinon

For a low-stress meal with ambience, choose one of the cafés on the photogenic place du Général de Gaulle. **Le Café des Arts** has great outdoor tables and a modern interior, and serves typical café fare (closed Wed, 4 rue Jean-Jacques Rousseau, tel. 02 47 93 09 84). But if food quality trumps outdoor ambience, try one of the next three restaurants.

La Treille Hôtel-Restaurant is a good choice for dining on regional dishes at fair prices inside or out (under its namesake trellis). Stéphanie offers a limited menu, but the cuisine is fresh, inventive, and delicious (*menus* from €19, closed Wed-Thu, good wine list, 4 place Jeanne d'Arc, tel. 02 47 93 07 71).

La Bonne France is sweet and simple, with homey and romantic seating indoors or in its quaint front yard. The chef, who excels at sauces, provides a fine budget *menu* selection (€15 for two courses, €19 for three, €26 for four, closed Wed, tel. 02 47 98 01 34).

L'Océanic, in the thick of the pedestrian zone, is where locals go for fish and tasty desserts. It has the best wine list in town, formal indoor or relaxed outdoor seating, and chic Marie-Poule to take your order (*menus* from €24, closed Sun-Mon, 13 rue Rabelais, tel. 02 47 93 44 55).

Restaurant-Musée Animé du Vin et de la Tonnellerie is a one-man show where jolly Dédé dishes up all the wine you can drink and *fouées* you can eat (little pastry shells filled with garlic paste, cheese, or *rillettes*—that's a meat spread), accompanied by *mâche*-and-walnut salad, green beans, dessert *fouées*, wine, and coffee—all for €19. Let your hair down in this get-to-know-your-neighbor kind of place as you watch Dédé slap the *fouées* in his rustic oven (daily for lunch and dinner, 12 rue Voltaire, tel. 02 47 93 25 63).

La Saladerie-Crêperie is a budget traveler's friend, with big salads and crêpes (€5-11) and *menus* from €10. There's good indoor and outdoor seating on traffic-free rue Rabelais (daily, #5, tel. 02 47 93 99 93).

Near Chinon

For a memorable countryside meal, drive 25 minutes to **Etape Gourmande at Domaine de la Giraudière,** in Villandry. A trip here combines well with visits to Villandry and Azay-le-Rideau.

Chinon Connections

By Minivan

From Chinon to Loire Châteaux: Acco-Dispo and **Quart de Tours** offer fixed-itinerary minivan excursions from Tours. Take the train to Tours from Chinon, or get several travelers together to book your own van from Chinon (see "Getting Around the Loire Valley" on page 5).

By Train

Twelve trains and SNCF buses link Chinon daily with the city of Tours (1 hour, connections to other châteaux and minibus excursions from Tours—see "Getting Around the Loire Valley" on page 5) and to the regional rail hub of St. Pierre-des-Corps in suburban Tours (TGV trains to distant destinations, and the fastest way to Paris). Traveling by train to the nearby châteaux (except for Azay-le-Rideau) requires a transfer in Tours and healthy walks from the stations to the châteaux. Fewer trains run on weekends.

From Chinon to Loire Châteaux: Azay-le-Rideau (7/day, 20 minutes direct, plus long walk to château), **Langeais** (5/day, 2 hours, transfer in Tours), **Amboise** (9/day, 1.5 hours, transfer in Tours), **Chenonceaux** (8/day, 1.5 hours, transfer in Tours), **Blois** (6/day, 2 hours, transfer in Tours and possibly in St. Pierre-des-Corps).

To Destinations Beyond the Loire: Paris' Gare Montparnasse (9/day, 2-2.5 hours, transfer in Tours and sometimes also St. Pierre-des-Corps), **Sarlat** (4/day, 5-6 hours, change at St. Pierre-des-Corps, then TGV to Libourne or Bordeaux-St. Jean, then train through Bordeaux vineyards to Sarlat), **Pontorson-Mont St. Michel** (3/day, 6 hours with change at Tours main station and Caen, then bus from Pontorson; or 8 hours via Paris TGV with changes at St. Pierre-des-Corps and Paris' Gare Montparnasse, then bus from Rennes), **Bayeux** (9/day, 5 hours with change in Caen and Tours, or 7 hours via Tours, St. Pierre-des-Corps, and Paris' Gare Montparnasse).

THE LOIRE

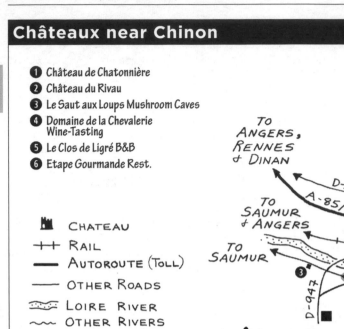

Châteaux near Chinon

1 Château de Chatonnière
2 Château du Rivau
3 Le Saut aux Loups Mushroom Caves
4 Domaine de la Chevalerie Wine-Tasting
5 Le Clos de Ligré B&B
6 Etape Gourmande Rest.

- CHATEAU
- RAIL
- AUTOROUTE (TOLL)
- OTHER ROADS
- LOIRE RIVER
- OTHER RIVERS
- RECOMMENDED BIKE ROUTE

10 MILES
10 KM

DCH

TO ANGERS, RENNES & DINAN
D-35
A-85/A-11
TO SAUMUR & ANGERS
TO SAUMUR
3
D-947
D-751
ABBAYE ROYALE DE FONTEVRAUD
TO LOUDON

Azay-le-Rideau

About 30 minutes west of Tours, Azay-le-Rideau (ah-zay luh ree-doh) is a pleasing little town with a small but lively pedestrian zone and a château that gets all the attention. Azay-le-Rideau works well as a base for visiting sights west of Tours by car, bike, or train (though the train station is a half-mile walk from the town center). It's also close to the A-85 autoroute, offering drivers reasonable access to châteaux near Amboise. Travelers who bed down here will be tempted by the fun sound-and-light show at the château.

Orientation to Azay-le-Rideau

Tourist Information

Azay-le-Rideau's TI is just below place de la République, a block to the right of the post office (July-Aug daily 10:00-19:00; Sept-Oct and April-June daily 9:00-13:00 & 14:00-18:00; Nov-March Mon-Sat 9:00-13:00 & 14:00-18:00, closed Sun; 4 rue du Château, tel. 02 47 45 44 40). Pick up information on the sound-and-light show, bike rentals, and summer buses to Villandry and Langeais.

Arrival in Azay-le-Rideau

It's about a 25-minute walk from the station to the town center (taxi mobile 06 60 94 42 00). Walk down from the station, turn left, and follow *Centre-Ville* signs. Drivers can head for the château and park there.

Sights in Azay-le-Rideau

▲▲Château d'Azay-le-Rideau

This charming 16th-century château, the fairy-tale castle of the Loire, sparkles on an island in the Indre River, its image romantically reflected in the slow-moving waters. The building is a prime example of an early-Renaissance château. With no defensive purpose, it was built simply for luxurious living in a luxurious setting. The ornamental facade is perfectly harmonious, and the interior—with its grand staircases and elegant loggias—is Italian-inspired.

The château was built from 1518 to 1527 by a filthy-rich banker—Gilles Berthelot, treasurer to the king of France. The structure has a delightfully feminine touch: Because Gilles was often away on work, his wife, Philippe, supervised the construction. The castle was so lavish that the king, François I, took note, giving it the ultimate compliment: He seized it, causing its owner to flee. Because this château survived the Revolution virtually unscathed, its interior capably demonstrates three centuries of royal styles. The French government purchased it in 1905.

Rooms are well-described in English, and a good audioguide gives even more information. For many, the highlight of a visit is the romantic garden, designed in the 19th century to show off the already beautiful château. Stroll around the entire building to enjoy romantic views from all sides, especially of the fanciful turrets, gracefully framed by the trees reflected on the water.

Cost and Hours: €8, audioguide-€4.50, daily July-Aug 9:30-19:00, April-June and Sept-Oct 9:30-18:00, Nov-March 10:00-12:30 & 14:00-17:30, last entry 45 minutes before closing, tel. 02 47 45 42 04, http://azay-le-rideau.monuments-nationaux.fr/en.

Sound-and-Light Show: The château hosts a sound-and-light show twice nightly in July and August (€10, gates open at 21:00, shows at 21:30 and 22:45). These shows allow you to meander through the grounds accompanied by flashy lighting and music.

Sleeping in Azay-le-Rideau

(€1 = about $1.40, country code: 33)
The town's appealing center may convince you to set up here (a good idea if you plan to see the sound-and-light show).

$$ Hôtel de Biencourt** is a find. Ideally located on a traffic-free street between place de la République (easy parking) and the château, this sharp boutique hotel is a former convent whose gentle owners have completed a masterful renovation. Rooms, including a few big family rooms, offer three-star comfort at two-star prices. There's a pleasing garden terrace and a cool lounge area (Db-€70, Tb-€86, Qb-€100, Wi-Fi, open March-mid-Nov, 7 rue de Balzac, tel. 02 47 45 20 75, fax 02 47 45 91 73, www.hotelbiencourt.com, biencourt@infonie.fr).

Eating in Azay-le-Rideau

Côte Cour is *the* place to dine for fresh and creative cuisine at reasonable prices. Friendly Sandra offers a limited menu, featuring local products and mostly organic foods, served in a warm interior or on a great outdoor terrace (€8.50 starters, €17 *plats*, closed Tue-Wed, faces the château gate at 19 rue Balzac, tel. 02 47 45 30 36). **Crêperie du Roy** is small, central, and cheap (24 rue Nationale, tel. 02 47 45 91 88). If you have a car, seriously consider the 10-minute drive to **Domaine de la Giraudière** in Villandry.

Azay-le-Rideau Connections

From Azay-le-Rideau, the **train** runs to **Tours** (8/day, 30 minutes, with connections to Langeais and other châteaux), to **Chinon** (7/day, 20 minutes), and to **Blois** (6/day, 1.75-2.5 hours, transfer in Tours and possibly in St. Pierre-des-Corps). Summertime **buses** run to Villandry and Langeais twice a day (the TI has bus schedules).

Langeais

One of the most imposing-looking fortresses of the Middle Ages,

Langeais—rated ▲—was built mostly for show. Towering above its appealing little village, it comes with a moat, a drawbridge, lavish defenses, and turrets.

Cost and Hours: €8.50, daily July-Aug 9:00-19:00, April-June and Sept-mid-Nov 9:30-18:30, mid-Nov-March 10:00-17:00, last entry one hour before closing, tel. 02 47 96 72 60, www.chateau-de-langeais.com.

Getting There: Nine trains a day link Langeais and **Tours** (20 minutes), with about five connections a day from there to **Chinon** (2 hours total, faster by bike). Drivers should turn right at the foot of the castle and follow the road left (around the castle) to find the parking lot (on the right). You can also find free parking a block from the château at a lot adjacent to the town market square.

Background: Langeais is located at a strategic point on the Loire River and the road to Tours (15 miles upstream), which for a time was the French capital. The only remaining part of the original castle is the thousand-year-old tower standing across from the castle's garden. (That castle, an English stronghold, was destroyed by the French king in the Hundred Years' War.)

The new castle, built in the 15th century, dates from the age of cannons, which would have made quick work of its tough-looking facade. In fact, the imposing walls were mostly for show. This is a transitional piece of architecture: part medieval and part Renaissance. The mullioned windows overlooking the courtyard indicate this was a fancy residence more than a defensive fortress. While Langeais makes a show of its defenses, castles built just 50 years later (such as Azay-le-Rideau) give not a hint of fortification.

Touring the Château: The interior is late-Middle Ages chic. It's the life's work of a 19th-century owner who was a lover of medieval art. He decorated and furnished the rooms with 15th- and 16th-century artifacts or good facsimiles. Most of what you see is modern-made in 16th-century style.

The palace is decked out as palaces were: designed to impress, and ready to pack and move. There were bedrooms for show and bedrooms for sleeping. The **banquet room** table would have groaned with food and luxury items—but just one long, communal napkin and no forks. Belgian tapestries on the walls still glimmer with 500-year-old silk thread. As you wander, notice how the rooms—with hanging tapestries, foldable chairs, and big chests with handles—could have been set up in a matter of hours. Big-time landowners circulated through their domains, moving every month or so.

In the so-called **Wedding Hall,** wax figures re-create the historic marriage that gave Langeais its 15 minutes of château fame. It was here that King Charles VIII secretly wed 14-year-old Anne (duchess of Brittany), a union that brought independent Brittany into France's fold. (An eight-minute sound-and-light show explains the event—usually in English at :15 past each hour.)

The top-floor museum has a rare series of 16th-century **tapestries** featuring nine heroes—biblical, Roman, and medieval. One of just three such sets in existence, seven of the original nine scenes survive.

Finish your visit by enjoying commanding **town views** from the ramparts.

Villandry

Villandry (vee-lahn-dree) is famous for its extensive gardens, considered to be the best in the Loire Valley. Its château is just
another Loire palace, but the grounds—arranged in elaborate geometric patterns and immaculately maintained—make it a ▲▲ sight (worth ▲▲▲ for gardeners). Still, if you're visiting anyway, it's worth three extra euros to tour the château as well.

Cost and Hours: €9.50, €6.50 for gardens only, daily April-Sept 9:00-19:00, March and Oct 9:00-18:00, Nov-Feb 9:00-17:00, tel. 02 47 50 02 09, www.chateauvillandry.com. Parking is free and easy between the trees across from the entry (but hide valuables in your trunk).

Background: Finished in 1536, Villandry was the last great Renaissance château built on the Loire. It's yet another pet project of a fabulously wealthy finance minister of François I—Jean le Breton. While serving as ambassador to Italy, Jean picked up a love of Italian Renaissance gardens. When he took over this property, he razed the 12th-century castle (keeping only the old tower), put up his own château, and installed a huge Italian-style garden. The château was purchased in 1906 by the present owner's great-grandfather, and the garden—a careful reconstruction of what the original might have been—is the result of three generations of passionate dedication.

Touring the Château and Gardens: An excellent English handout included with your admission leads you through the **château**'s elegant 19th-century rooms. They feel so lived-in that you'll wonder if the family just stepped out to get their poodle bathed. The 15-minute *Four Seasons of Villandry* slideshow (with period music and no narration) offers a look at the gardens throughout the year in a relaxing little theater. The literal high point of your château visit is the spiral climb to the top of the keep—the only surviving part of the medieval castle—where you'll find a grand view of the gardens and surrounding countryside.

The lovingly tended **gardens** are well-described by your handout. Follow its recommended route through the four garden types. The 10-acre Renaissance garden, inspired by the 1530s Italian-style original, is full of symbolism. Even the herb and vegetable sections are put together with artistic flair. The earliest Loire gardens were practical, grown by medieval abbey monks who needed vegetables to feed their community and medicinal herbs to cure their ailments. And those monks liked geometrical patterns. Later Italian influence brought decorative ponds, tunnels, and fountains. Harmonizing the flowers and vegetables was an innovation of 16th-century Loire châteaux. This example is the closest we have to that garden style. The 85,000 plants—half of which come from the family greenhouse—are replanted twice a year by 10 full-time gardeners. The place is as manicured as a putting green—just try to find a weed. Stroll under the grapevine trellis, through a good-looking salad zone, and among Anjou pears (from the nearby region of Angers). Charts posted throughout identify everything in English.

Bring bread for the piranha-like carp who prowl the fanciful moat. Like the carp swimming around other Loire châteaux, they're so voracious, they'll gather at your feet to frantically eat your spit.

You can stay as late as you like in the gardens, though you must enter before the ticket office closes.

Eating and Sleeping in Villandry

The pleasant little village of Villandry offers several cafés and restaurants, a small grocery store, a bakery, and good rates at the nice little **$$ Hôtel-Restaurant le Cheval Rouge**** (Db-€60-70, Tb-€70-80, Qb-€90-100, dinner *menus* from €20, tel. 02 47 50 02 07, www.lecheval-rouge.com).

Eating near Villandry

Etape Gourmande at Domaine de la Giraudière offers a rustic farmhouse dining experience. Owner Beatrice provides great service and country-good cuisine from her limited menu (ask her how she landed here). The *salade gourmande* makes a good lunch or a hearty first course for dinner (consider splitting it). The *cochon au lait* (melt-in-your-mouth pork, not available in summer) and the nougat dessert are also tasty (€17-33 *menus*, mid-March-mid-Nov daily 12:00-15:00 & 19:30-21:00, closed mid-Nov-mid-March, a half-mile from Villandry's château toward Druye, tel. 02 47 50 08 60, fax 02 47 50 06 60). This place works best for lunch, as it's between Villandry and Azay-le-Rideau. It also works for dinner when combined with a visit to Azay-le-Rideau's sound-and-light show.

More Château Gardens

Gardeners will be tempted by these untouristy "lesser châteaux" because of their pleasing plantings.

Château de Chatonnière—The grounds feature romantic paths through exquisitely tended gardens of various themes. Surrounded

by fields of wildflowers (my favorite part), it's a must-visit for gardeners and flower fanatics in May to early July, when the place positively explodes in fragrance and color. At other times, when flowers are few, the entry fee is not worth it for most.

Cost and Hours: €6, mid-March-mid-Nov daily 10:00-19:00, château interior closed to visitors, between Langeais and Azay-le-Rideau just off D-57, tel. 02 47 45 40 29, www.lachatonniere.com.

Château du Rivau—Gleaming-white and medieval, this château lies wedged between wheat and sunflower fields, and makes for a memorable 15-minute drive from Chinon. Its owners have spared little expense in their 20-year renovation of the 15th-century castle and its extensive gardens. The 14 different flower and vegetable gardens and orchards are kid-friendly (with elf and fairy guides) and lovingly tended with art installations, topiaries, hammocks, birds, a maze, and much more. The stables—with projections about jousting and "Heroic Horses" from history—will delight most kids (English subtitles), but the medieval castle interior is skippable. A good little café serves reasonable meals in a lovely setting.

Cost and Hours: €10, daily April-Sept 10:00-18:00, Oct-mid-Nov 10:00-12:30 & 14:00-18:00, closed mid-Nov-March; in Lémeré on D-759—from Chinon follow *Richelieu* signs, then signs to the château; tel. 02 47 95 77 47, www.chateaudurivau.com.

Ussé

This château, famous as an inspiration for Charles Perrault's classic version of the Sleeping Beauty story, is worth a quick photo stop for its fairy-tale turrets and gardens, but don't bother touring the interior of this pricey pearl. The best view, with reflections and a golden-slipper picnic spot, is from just across the bridge.

Cost and Hours: €13, daily April-Aug 10:00-19:00, mid-Feb-March and Sept-mid-Nov 10:00-18:00, closed mid-Nov-mid-Feb, tel. 02 47 95 54 05, www.chateaudusse.fr.

THE LOIRE

Abbaye Royale de Fontevraud

The Royal Abbey of Fontevraud (fohn-tuh-vroh) is a 15-minute journey west from Chinon. This vast 12th-century abbey provides a fascinating look at medieval monastic life. The "abbey" was actually a 12th-century monastic city, the largest such compound in Europe—with four monastic complexes, all within a fortified wall.

Cost and Hours: €9, audioguide-daily 9:30-18:30, July-Aug until 19:30, closed Jan, tel. 02 41 51 73 52, www.abbayedefontevraud.com. Spring for the helpful €4 audioguide (the free English leaflet gives light coverage). There's a free parking lot 100 yards beyond the abbey entrance.

Background: The order of Fontevraud, founded in 1101, was an experiment of rare audacity. This was a double monastery, where both men and women lived under the authority of an abbess while observing the rules of St. Benedict (but influenced by the cult of the Virgin Mary). Men and women lived separately and chastely within the abbey walls. The order thrived, and in the 16th century, this was the administrative head of more than 150 monasteries. Four communities lived within these walls until the Revolution. In 1804, Napoleon made the abbey a prison, which actually helped preserve the building. It functioned as a prison for 150 years, until 1963, with five wooden floors filled with cells. Designed to house 800 inmates, the prison was notoriously harsh. Life expectancy here was eight months.

Touring the Abbey: Thanks to the €4 audioguide, this abbey is well-presented for English speakers.

Your visit begins in the bright, 12th-century, Romanesque **abbey church.** Sit on the steps, savor the ethereal light and the cavernous setting, and gaze down the nave. At the end of it are four painted sarcophagi belonging to Eleanor of Aquitaine; her second husband, Henry II, the first of the Plantagenet kings; their son Richard the Lionhearted; and his sister-in-law. These are the tops of the sarcophagi only. Even though we know these Plantagenets were buried here (because they gave lots of money to the abbey), no one knows the fate of the actual bodies.

You'll leave the church through the right transept into the **cloister.** This was the center of the abbey, where the nuns read, exercised, checked their email, and washed their hands. While visiting the abbey, remember that monastic life was very simple: nothing but prayers, readings, and work. Daily rations were a loaf of bread and a half-liter of wine per person, plus soup and smoked fish.

Next you'll find the **chapter house,** where the nuns' meetings took place, as well as the **community room**— the only heated room in the abbey, where the nuns embroidered linen. In rooms leading off the cloister, Renaissance paintings feature portraits of the women in black habits who ran this abbey.

The nearby **refectory,** built to feed 400 silent monks at a time, was later the prison work yard, where inmates built wooden chairs.

Your abbey visit ends in the honeycombed 12th-century **kitchen,** with five bays covered by 18 chimneys to evacuate smoke. It likely served as a smokehouse for fish farmed in the abbey ponds. Abbeys like this were industrious places, but focused on self-sufficiency rather than trade.

Finish your visit by wandering through the abbey's **medicinal gardens** out back.

Near Fontevraud: Mushroom Caves

For an unusual fungus find close to the abbey of Fontevraud, visit the mushroom caves at **Le Saut aux Loups.** France is the world's third-largest producer of mushrooms (after the US and China). Climb to a cliff ledge and visit 16 chilly rooms bored into limestone to discover everything about the care and nurturing of mushrooms. You'll see them raised in planters, plastic bags, logs, and straw bales, and you'll learn about their incubation, pasteurization, and fermentation. Abandoned limestone quarries like this are fertile homes for mushroom cultivation, and have made the Loire Valley the king of mushrooms in France since the late 1800s. You'll ogle at the weird shapes and never take your 'shrooms for granted again. The growers harvest a ton of mushrooms a month in these caves; shitakes are their most important crop. Pick up the English booklet and follow the fungus. Many visitors come only for the on-site mushroom restaurant, whose wood-fired *galipettes* (stuffed mushrooms with crème fraiche and herbs) are the kitchen's forté.

Cost and Hours: €6, March-Nov daily 10:00-18:00, closed Dec-Feb; lunch served daily except Tue—weekends only in off-season; dress warmly, just north of Fontevraud at Montsoreau's west end along the river, tel. 02 41 51 70 30, www.troglo-sautaux loups.com.

Sleeping and Eating near Abbaye Royale de Fontevraud

(€1 = about $1.40, country code: 33)
$$$ Hôtel la Croix Blanche**,** 10 steps from the abbey, welcomes travelers with open terraces and will have you sleeping and dining

in comfort. This ambitious restaurant-hotel combines a hunting-lodge feel with polished service, comfortable open spaces, a pool, and 23 rooms with classic French decor (Db-€90-130, Db suites-€100-150, free Wi-Fi, place Plantagenets, tel. 02 41 51 71 11, fax 02 41 38 15 38, www.hotel-croixblanche.com, info@hotel-croixblanche.com).

The abbey faces the main square of a cute town with several handy eateries. The *boulangerie* opposite the entrance to the abbey serves mouthwatering quiche and sandwiches at impossibly good prices. You'll also find a few *crêperies* and cafés near the abbey.

PRACTICALITIES

This section covers just the basics on traveling in France (for much more information, see the latest edition of *Rick Steves' France*). You can find free advice on specific topics at www.ricksteves.com/tips.

The Language

In France, it's essential to acknowledge the person before getting down to business. Start any conversation, or enter any shop, by saying: "*Bonjour, madame (or monsieur).*" To ask if they speak English, say, "*Parlez-vous anglais?*", and hope they speak more English than you speak French. See "Survival Phrases" at the end of this chapter.

Money

France uses the euro currency: 1 euro (€) = about $1.40. To convert prices in euros to dollars, add about 40 percent: €20 = about $28, €50 = about $70. (Check www.oanda.com for the latest exchange rates.)

The standard way for travelers to get euros is to withdraw money from a cash machine (called a *distributeur* in France) using a debit card, ideally with a Visa or MasterCard logo. Before departing, call your bank or credit-card company: Confirm that your card(s) will work overseas, find out the PIN code for your credit card, ask about international transaction fees, and alert them that you'll be making withdrawals in Europe.

To keep your valuables safe, wear a money belt. But if you do lose your credit or debit card, report the loss immediately to the respective global customer-assistance centers. Call these 24-hour US numbers collect: Visa (410/581-9994), MasterCard (636/722-7111), and American Express (623/492-8427). In France, to make a collect call to the US, dial 00 00 11 to reach an international operator.

Dealing with "Chip and PIN": France (and much of northern Europe) is adopting a "chip-and-PIN" system for credit cards. These "smartcards" come with an embedded microchip, and cardholders enter a PIN code instead of signing a receipt. If your US card is rejected at a store, a cashier will probably be able to process your card the old-fashioned way. A few merchants might insist on the PIN code—making it helpful for you to know the code for your credit card (ask your credit-card company). The easiest solution is to pay for your purchases with cash you've withdrawn from an ATM. Your US credit card probably won't work at France's automated pay points, such as ticket machines at train and subway stations, toll booths, parking garages, luggage lockers, and self-serve pumps at gas stations. But in many of these cases, a cash-only payment option is available.

Phoning

Smart travelers use the telephone to reserve or reconfirm rooms, reserve restaurants, get directions, research transportation connections, confirm tour times, phone home, and lots more.

To call France from the US or Canada: Dial 011-33 and then the local number, omitting the initial zero. (The 011 is our international access code, and 33 is France's country code.)

To call France from a European country: Dial 00-33 followed by the local number, omitting the initial zero. (The 00 is Europe's international access code.)

To call within France: Just dial the local number (including the initial zero).

To call from France to another country: Dial 00 followed by the country code (for example, 1 for the US or Canada), then the area code and number. If you're calling European countries whose phone numbers begin with 0, you'll usually have to omit that 0 when you dial.

Tips on Phoning: To make calls in France, you can buy two different types of phone cards—international or insertable—sold locally at newsstands. Cheap international phone cards (*cartes à code*; pronounced cart ah code), which work with a scratch-to-reveal PIN code at any phone, allow you to call home to the US for pennies a minute, and also work for domestic calls within France. Insertable phone cards (*télécarte*; tay-lay-kart), which must be inserted into public pay phones, are reasonable for calls within France (and work for international calls as well, but not as cheaply as the international phone cards). Calling from your hotel-room phone is usually expensive, unless you use an international phone card. A mobile phone—whether an American one that works in

France, or a European one you buy when you arrive—is handy, but can be pricey. For more on phoning, see www.ricksteves.com/phoning.

Making Hotel Reservations

To ensure the best value, I recommend reserving rooms in advance, particularly during peak season. Email the hotelier with the following key pieces of information: number and type of rooms; number of nights; date of arrival; date of departure; and any special requests. (For a sample form, see www.ricksteves.com/reservation.) Use the European style for writing dates: day/month/year. For example, for a two-night stay in July, you could request: "1 double room for 2 nights, arrive 16/07/12, depart 18/07/12." Hoteliers typically ask for your credit-card number as a deposit.

In these times of economic uncertainty, some hotels are willing to deal to attract guests—try emailing several to ask their best price. In general, hotel prices can soften if you do any of the following: offer to pay cash, stay at least three nights, mention this book, or travel off-season. You can also try asking for a cheaper room (for example, with a bathroom down the hall), or offer to skip breakfast.

The French have a simple hotel-rating system based on amenities (zero through five stars, indicated in this book by * through *****). Two-star hotels are my mainstay. Other accommodation options include bed-and-breakfasts (*chambres d'hôtes*, usually more affordable than hotels), hostels, campgrounds, or even homes (*gîtes*, rented by the week).

Eating

The cuisine is a highlight of any French adventure. It's sightseeing for your palate. For a formal meal, go to a restaurant. If you want the option of lighter fare (just soup or a sandwich), head for a café or brasserie instead.

French restaurants usually open for dinner at 19:00 and are typically most crowded around 20:30. Last seating is usually about 21:00 or 22:00 (earlier in villages). If a restaurant serves lunch, it generally goes from about 11:30 to 14:00.

In France, an entrée is the first course, and *le plat* or *le plat du jour* is the main course with vegetables. If you ask for the *menu* (muh-noo), you won't get a list of dishes; you'll get a fixed-price meal—usually your choice of three courses (soup, appetizer, or salad; main course with vegetables; and cheese course or dessert). Drinks are extra. Ask for *la carte* (lah kart) if you want to see a menu and order à la carte, like the locals do. Request the waiter's help in deciphering the French.

Cafés and brasseries provide budget-friendly meals. If you're hungry between lunch and dinner, when restaurants are closed, go to a brasserie, which generally serves throughout the day. (Some cafés do as well, but others close their kitchens from 14:00 to 18:00.) Compared to restaurants, cafés and brasseries usually have more limited and inexpensive fare, including salads, sandwiches, omelets, *plats du jour*, and more. Check the price list first, which by law must be posted prominently. There are two sets of prices: You'll pay more for the same drink if you're seated at a table *(salle)* than if you're seated at the bar or counter *(comptoir)*.

A 12-15 percent service charge *(service compris)* is always included in the bill. Most French never tip, but if you feel the service was exceptional, it's kind to tip up to 5 percent extra.

Transportation

By Train: Travelers who need to cover long distances in France by train can get a good deal with a France Railpass, sold only outside Europe. To see if a railpass could save you money, check www.ricksteves.com/rail. To research train schedules, visit Germany's excellent all-Europe website, http://bahn.hafas.de/bin/query.exe/en, or France's SNCF (national railroad) site, www.sncf.fr.

You can buy tickets at train-station ticket windows, SNCF boutiques (small, centrally located offices of the national rail company), and travel agencies.

You are required to validate (*composter*, kohm-poh-stay) all train tickets and reservations; before boarding look for a yellow machine to stamp your ticket or reservation. Strikes *(grève)* in France are common but generally last no longer than a day or two; ask your hotelier if one is coming.

By Car: It's cheaper to arrange most car rentals from the US. For tips on your insurance options, see www.ricksteves.com/cdw, and for route planning, try www.viamichelin.com. Bring your driver's license. France's freeway (*autoroute*) system is slick and speedy, but pricey; four hours of driving costs about €25 in tolls (pay cash, since US credit cards won't work in the machines). A car is a worthless headache in cities—park it safely (get tips from your hotel or pay to park at well-patrolled lots; look for blue *P* signs). As break-ins are common, be sure all of your valuables are out of sight and locked in the trunk, or even better, with you or in your hotel room.

Helpful Hints

Pickpocket Alert: France has hardworking pickpockets. Assume beggars are pickpockets and any scuffle is simply a distraction by a team of thieves. If you stop for any commotion or show, put your hands in your pockets before someone else does. Better yet, wear a money belt.

Emergency Help: For English-speaking **police** help, dial 17. To summon an **ambulance,** call 15. To replace a passport, go in person to the **US Consulate and Embassy** in Paris (tel. 01 43 12 22 22, passport services open Mon–Fri 9:00-11:00, closed Sat–Sun, 4 avenue Gabriel, Mo: Concorde, http://france.usembassy.gov) or other **US Consulates** (Lyon: tel. 04 78 38 36 88; Marseille: tel. 04 91 54 92 00; Nice: tel. 04 93 88 89 55; Strasbourg: tel. 03 88 35 31 04; Bordeaux: tel. 05 56 48 63 85); or the **Canadian Consulate and Embassy** in Paris (tel. 01 44 43 29 00, reception open daily 9:00-12:00 & 14:00–17:00, 35 avenue Montaigne, Mo: Franklin D. Roosevelt, www.amb-canada.fr) or other **Canadian Consulates** (Lyon: tel. 04 78 38 33 03; Nice: tel. 04 93 92 93 22). For more information on what to do in case of theft or loss, see www.rick steves.com/help. For other concerns, get advice from your hotelier.

Time: France uses the 24-hour clock. It's the same through 12:00 noon, then keep going: 13:00, 14:00, and so on. France, like most of continental Europe, is six/nine hours ahead of the East/West Coasts of the US.

Business Hours: Most shops are open from Monday through Saturday (generally 10:00–12:00 & 14:00–19:00) and closed on Sunday, though some grocery stores and bakeries are open Sunday morning until noon. In smaller towns, some businesses are closed on Monday until 14:00 and sometimes all day. Touristy shops are usually open daily.

Sights: Opening and closing hours of sights can change unexpectedly; confirm the latest times with the local tourist information office or its website. Some major churches enforce a modest dress code (no bare shoulders or shorts) for everyone, even children.

Holidays and Festivals: France celebrates many holidays, which can close sights and attract crowds (book hotel rooms ahead). For information on holidays and festivals, check France's website: www.franceguide.com. For a simple list showing major—though not all—events, see www.ricksteves.com/festivals.

Numbers and Stumblers: What Americans call the second floor of a building is the first floor in Europe. Europeans write dates as day/month/year, so Christmas is 25/12/12. Commas are decimal points and vice versa—a dollar and a half is 1,50, a thousand is 1.000, and there are 5.280 feet in a mile. France uses the metric system: A kilogram is 2.2 pounds; a liter is about a quart; and a kilometer is six-tenths of a mile.

Resources from Rick Steves

This Snapshot guide is excerpted from the latest edition of *Rick Steves' France,* which is one of more than 30 titles in my series of guidebooks on European travel. I also produce a public television series, *Rick Steves' Europe,* and a public radio show, *Travel with*

Rick Steves. My website, www.ricksteves.com, offers free travel information, a Graffiti Wall for travelers' comments, guidebook updates, my travel blog, an online travel store, and information on European railpasses and our tours of Europe. If you're bringing a mobile device on your trip, you can download free information from Rick Steves Audio Europe, featuring podcasts of my radio shows, free audio tours of major sights in Europe, and travel interviews about France (via www.ricksteves.com/audioeurope, iTunes, or the Rick Steves Audio Europe free smartphone app).

Additional Resources
Tourist Information: www.franceguide.com
Passports and Red Tape: www.travel.state.gov
Packing List: www.ricksteves.com/packlist
Travel Insurance: www.ricksteves.com/insurance
Cheap Flights: www.skyscanner.net
Airplane Carry-on Restrictions: www.tsa.gov/travelers
Updates for This Book: www.ricksteves.com/update

How Was Your Trip?
If you'd like to share your tips, concerns, and discoveries after using this book, please fill out the survey at www.ricksteves.com/feedback. Thanks in advance—it helps a lot.

French Survival Phrases

When using the phonetics, try to nasalize the n̲ sound.

Good day.	**Bonjour.**	boh̲n-zhoor
Mrs. / Mr.	**Madame / Monsieur**	mah-dahm / muhs-yur
Do you speak English?	**Parlez-vous anglais?**	par-lay-voo ah̲n-glay
Yes. / No.	**Oui. / Non.**	wee / noh̲n
I understand.	**Je comprends.**	zhuh koh̲n-prah̲n
I don't understand.	**Je ne comprends pas.**	zhuh nuh koh̲n-prah̲n pah
Please.	**S'il vous plaît.**	see voo play
Thank you.	**Merci.**	mehr-see
I'm sorry.	**Désolé.**	day-zoh-lay
Excuse me.	**Pardon.**	par-doh̲n
(No) problem.	**(Pas de) problème.**	(pah duh) proh-blehm
It's good.	**C'est bon.**	say boh̲n
Goodbye.	**Au revoir.**	oh vwahr
one / two	**un / deux**	uh̲n / duh
three / four	**trois / quatre**	twah / kah-truh
five / six	**cinq / six**	sa̲nk / sees
seven / eight	**sept / huit**	seht / weet
nine / ten	**neuf / dix**	nuhf / dees
How much is it?	**Combien?**	koh̲n-bee-a̲n
Write it?	**Ecrivez?**	ay-kree-vay
Is it free?	**C'est gratuit?**	say grah-twee
Included?	**Inclus?**	a̲n-klew
Where can I buy / find...?	**Où puis-je acheter / trouver...?**	oo pwee-zhuh ah-shuh-tay / troo-vay
I'd like / We'd like...	**Je voudrais / Nous voudrions...**	zhuh voo-dray / noo voo-dree-oh̲n
...a room.	**...une chambre.**	ewn shah̲n-bruh
...a ticket to ___.	**...un billet pour ___.**	uh̲n bee-yay poor
Is it possible?	**C'est possible?**	say poh-see-bluh
Where is...?	**Où est...?**	oo ay
...the train station	**...la gare**	lah gar
...the bus station	**...la gare routière**	lah gar root-yehr
...tourist information	**...l'office du tourisme**	loh-fees dew too-reez-muh
Where are the toilets?	**Où sont les toilettes?**	oo soh̲n lay twah-leht
men	**hommes**	ohm
women	**dames**	dahm
left / right	**à gauche / à droite**	ah gohsh / ah dwaht
straight	**tout droit**	too dwah
When does this open / close?	**Ça ouvre / ferme à quelle heure?**	sah oo-vruh / fehrm ah kehl ur
At what time?	**À quelle heure?**	ah kehl ur
Just a moment.	**Un moment.**	uh̲n moh-mah̲n
now / soon / later	**maintenant / bientôt / plus tard**	ma̲n-tuh-nah̲n / bee-a̲n-toh / plew tar
today / tomorrow	**aujourd'hui / demain**	oh-zhoor-dwee / duh-ma̲n

In a French Restaurant

I'd like / We'd like...	Je voudrais / Nous voudrions...	zhuh voo-dray / noo voo-dree-ohn
...to reserve...	...réserver...	ray-zehr-vay
...a table for one / two.	...une table pour un / deux.	ewn tah-bluh poor uhn / duh
Non-smoking.	Non fumeur.	nohn few-mur
Is this seat free?	C'est libre?	say lee-bruh
The menu (in English), please.	La carte (en anglais), s'il vous plaît.	lah kart (ahn ahn-glay) see voo play
service (not) included	service (non) compris	sehr-vees (nohn) kohn-pree
to go	à emporter	ah ahn-por-tay
with / without	avec / sans	ah-vehk / sahn
and / or	et / ou	ay / oo
special of the day	plat du jour	plah dew zhoor
specialty of the house	spécialité de la maison	spay-see-ah-lee-tay duh lah may-zohn
appetizers	hors-d'oeuvre	or-duh-vruh
first course (soup, salad)	entrée	ahn-tray
main course (meat, fish)	plat principal	plah pran-see-pahl
bread	pain	pan
cheese	fromage	froh-mahzh
sandwich	sandwich	sahnd-weech
soup	soupe	soop
salad	salade	sah-lahd
meat	viande	vee-ahnd
chicken	poulet	poo-lay
fish	poisson	pwah-sohn
seafood	fruits de mer	frwee duh mehr
fruit	fruit	frwee
vegetables	légumes	lay-gewm
dessert	dessert	duh-sehr
mineral water	eau minérale	oh mee-nay-rahl
tap water	l'eau du robinet	loh dew roh-bee-nay
milk	lait	lay
(orange) juice	jus (d'orange)	zhew (doh-rahnzh)
coffee	café	kah-fay
tea	thé	tay
wine	vin	van
red / white	rouge / blanc	roozh / blahn
glass / bottle	verre / bouteille	vehr / boo-teh-ee
beer	bière	bee-ehr
Cheers!	Santé!	sahn-tay
More. / Another.	Plus. / Un autre.	plew / uhn oh-truh
The same.	La même chose.	lah mehm shohz
The bill, please.	L'addition, s'il vous plaît.	lah-dee-see-ohn see voo play
tip	pourboire	poor-bwar
Delicious!	Délicieux!	day-lee-see-uh

For more user-friendly French phrases, check out *Rick Steves' French Phrase Book and Dictionary* or *Rick Steves' French, Italian & German Phrase Book*.

INDEX

INDEX

INDEX

Audio Europe

▶ Plan Your Trip

Browse thousands of articles and a wealth of money-saving tips for planning your dream trip. You'll find up-to-date information on Europe's best destinations, packing smart, getting around, finding rooms, staying healthy, avoiding scams and more.

▶ Eurail Passes

Find out, step-by-step, if a railpass makes sense for your trip—and how to avoid buying more than you need. Get free shipping on online orders

▶ Graffiti Wall & Travelers Helpline

Learn, ask, share—our online community of savvy travelers is a great resource for first-time travelers to Europe, as well as seasoned pros.

Rick Steves®

www.ricksteves.com

EUROPE GUIDES

Best of Europe
Eastern Europe
Europe Through the Back Door
Mediterranean Cruise Ports

COUNTRY GUIDES

Croatia & Slovenia
England
France
Germany
Great Britain
Ireland
Italy
Portugal
Scandinavia
Spain
Switzerland

CITY & REGIONAL GUIDES

Amsterdam, Bruges & Brussels
Budapest
Florence & Tuscany
Greece: Athens & the Peloponnese
Istanbul
London
Paris
Prague & the Czech Republic
Provence & the French Riviera
Rome
Venice
Vienna, Salzburg & Tirol

SNAPSHOT GUIDES

Barcelona
Berlin
Bruges & Brussels
Copenhagen & the Best of Denmark
Dublin
Dubrovnik
Hill Towns of Central Italy
Italy's Cinque Terre
Krakow, Warsaw & Gdansk
Lisbon
Madrid & Toledo
Munich, Bavaria & Salzburg
Naples & the Amalfi Coast
Northern Ireland
Norway
Scotland
Sevilla, Granada & Southern Spain
Stockholm

POCKET GUIDES

London
Paris
Rome

TRAVEL CULTURE

Europe 101
European Christmas
Postcards from Europe
Travel as a Political Act

Rick Steves guidebooks are published by Avalon Travel,
a member of the Perseus Books Group.

NOW AVAILABLE:
eBOOKS, APPS & BLU-RAY

eBOOKS

Most guides are available as eBooks from Amazon, Barnes & Noble, Borders, Apple, and Sony. Free apps for eBook reading are available in the Apple App Store and Android Market, and eBook readers such as Kindle, Nook, and Kobo all have free apps that work on smartphones.

RICK STEVES' EUROPE DVDs

10 New Shows 2011-2012
Austria & the Alps
Eastern Europe
England & Wales
European Christmas
European Travel Skills & Specials
France
Germany, BeNeLux & More
Greece & Turkey
Iran
Ireland & Scotland
Italy's Cities
Italy's Countryside
Scandinavia
Spain
Travel Extras

BLU-RAY

Celtic Charms
Eastern Europe Favorites
European Christmas
Italy Through the Back Door
Mediterranean Mosaic
Surprising Cities of Europe

PHRASE BOOKS & DICTIONARIES

French
French, Italian & German
German
Italian
Portuguese
Spanish

JOURNALS

Rick Steves' Pocket Travel Journal
Rick Steves' Travel Journal

APPS

Select Rick Steves guides are available as apps in the Apple App Store.

PLANNING MAPS

Britain, Ireland & London
Europe
France & Paris
Germany, Austria & Switzerland
Ireland
Italy
Spain & Portugal

Rick Steves books and DVDs are available at bookstores and through online booksellers.

Avalon Travel
a member of the Perseus Books Group
1700 Fourth Street
Berkeley, California 94710

Text © 2011, 2009, 2008, 2007, 2006, 2005, 2004, 2003, 2002, 2001, 2000 by Rick Steves
and Steve Smith. All rights reserved. Maps © 2011, 2009, 2008 by Europe Through the
Back Door. All rights reserved. Paris Métro map © 2010 by La Régie Autonome des
Transports Parisiens (RATP).
Used with permission.
Portions of this book originally appeared in *Rick Steves' France 2012*.

Printed in Canada by Friesens. First printing January 2012.

ISBN 978-1-61238-357-6

For the latest on Rick's lectures, guidebooks, tours, public radio show, and public television
series, contact Europe Through the Back Door, Box 2009, Edmonds, WA 98020, 425/771-
8303, fax 425/771-0833, rick@ricksteves.com, www.ricksteves.com.

Europe Through the Back Door Reviewing Editors: Cameron Hewitt, Jennifer Madison
  Davis
ETBD Editors: Tom Griffin, Gretchen Strauch, Suzanne Kotz, Cathy McDonald, Cathy
  Lu, Samantha Oberholzer, Candace Winegrad
ETBD Managing Editor: Risa Laib
Research Assistance: Kristin Kusnic Michel, Caitlin Woodbury, Rolinka Bloeming
Avalon Travel Senior Editor and Series Manager: Madhu Prasher
Avalon Travel Project Editor: Kelly Lydick
Copy Editor: Naomi Adler Dancis
Proofreader: Becca Freed
Indexer: Stephen Callahan
Production and Layout: McGuire Barber Design
Cover Design: Kimberly Glyder Design
Graphic Content Director: Laura VanDeventer
Maps & Graphics: David C. Hoerlein, Laura VanDeventer, Lauren Mills, Twozdai Hulse,
  Barb Geisler, Mike Morgenfeld, Kat Bennett, Brice Ticen
Front Cover Photo: Azay-le-Rideau © Rick Steves
Title Page Photo: Amboise © Francesco Bucchi/www.123rf.com
Page V Photo: Statue of Louis XII at Blois castle, Loire, France © netrun78/www.123rf.com
Page 1 Photo: Royal french castle Chambord © Alexander Sorokopud/www.123rf.com
Additional Photography: Rick Steves, Steve Smith, David C. Hoerlein, Cameron Hewitt,
  Dominic Bonuccelli, Laura VanDeventer, Lauren Mills, Gretchen Strauch, Rich Earl,
  Julie Coen, Barb Geisler, Robyn Cronin, Michaelanne Jerome, Abe Bringolf, Mary Ann
  Cameron, Paul Orcutt, Michael Potter, Carol Ries, Dorian Yates, Rob Unck, Wikimedia
  Commons, Rachel Worthman pg. 32

Want More France?

Maximize the experience with Rick Steves as your guide

Guidebooks
Provence and Paris guides make side-trips smooth and affordable

Phrase Books
Rely on Rick's French Phrase Book and Dictionary

Rick's DVDs
Preview your destinations with 8 shows on France

Rick's Audio Europe™ App
Free audio tours for Paris' top sights

Small-Group Tours
Rick offers 8 great itineraries through France

For all the details, visit ricksteves.com

ABOUT THE AUTHORS

RICK STEVES

 Since 1973, Rick Steves has spent 100 days every year exploring Europe. Rick produces a public television series *(Rick Steves' Europe)*, a public radio show *(Travel with Rick Steves)*, and an app and podcast *(Rick Steves Audio Europe)*; writes a bestselling series of guidebooks and a nationally syndicated newspaper column; organizes guided tours that take over ten thousand travelers to Europe annually; and offers an information-packed website (www.ricksteves.com). With the help of his hardworking staff of 80 at Europe Through the Back Door—in Edmonds, Washington, just north of Seattle—Rick's mission is to make European travel fun, affordable, and culturally enlightening for Americans.

STEVE SMITH

Steve Smith manages tour planning for Rick Steves' Europe Through the Back Door and has been researching guidebooks with Rick for two decades. Fluent in French, he's lived in France on several occasions, starting when he was seven, and has traveled there annually since 1986. Steve's wife, Karen Lewis Smith, who's an expert on French cuisine and wine, provides invaluable contributions to his books, as do his two children.